# *Perfect*
# MANNERS

# *Perfect* MANNERS

## HOW YOU SHOULD BEHAVE SO YOUR HORSE DOES TOO

# KELLY MARKS

EBURY PRESS LONDON

First published in Great Britain in 2002
1 3 5 7 9 10 8 6 4 2

Text © Kelly Marks 2002
Photographs © Jess Wallace and Jane Young

Ebury Press
Random House, 20 Vauxhall Bridge Road, London SW1V 2SA

Random House Australia (Pty) Limited
20 Alfred Street, Milsons Point, Sydney, New South Wales 2061, Australia

Random House New Zealand Limited
18 Poland Road, Glenfield, Auckland 10, New Zealand

Random House (Pty) Limited
Endulini, 5a Jubilee Road, Parktown 2193, South Africa

The Random House Group Limited Reg. No. 954009
www.randomhouse.co.uk

Papers used by Ebury Press are natural, recyclable products made from wood
grown in sustainable forests.

A CIP catalogue record for this book is available from the British Library

ISBN 0 09 188270 2

Editor: Emma Callery
Designer: Alison Shackleton
Photographs: all photographs are the property of Jess Wallace and Jane Young
with the exception of those on pages 6 and 28 (David Millar), 18 (Kelly Marks),
32, 33, 38, 165 and 168 (Linda Ruffle), 211 (Diana Maclean) and 221 (Paul Foxley).

Printed and bound by Tien Wah Press in Singapore

# CONTENTS

# INTRODUCTION

It isn't too much of a surprise that I'm now spending my life helping horses and people understand one another. My father being a racehorse trainer meant I was brought up around horses. When he was 17 years of age my father won two classic races on Godiva, a filly previously thought unrideable. The idea of building such a special relationship with a horse became a rather romantic ideal and I considered myself a 'deprived child' not getting my own pony until I was all of 11 years old. However, that Seamus turned out to be the most beautiful little grey pony in the world (to me) did a lot to make up for it. Soon, thanks to Seamus and the invaluable support of my sister, Sandra, I became quite a 'useful commodity' for a teenager, riding for dealers to show off their horses to best advantage.

I later went on to ride in races, which brought me even closer to horses. This closeness was probably what made me decide in

**KELLY MARKS AND MONTY ROBERTS**

WHEN THE STUDENT IS READY, THE TEACHER WILL APPEAR.

my last four years of racing that I didn't like using the whip any more, so I simply stopped using it. You wouldn't have thought this was the brightest career move for a competitive rider but, in fact, I had my biggest career successes in that time.

Coincidentally (or whatever happens to be your belief in these matters), while I was making choices like this there was a man on another continent of whom I'd never heard who was coming to the same conclusions. I was to have a chance meeting with this man, Monty Roberts, known to many as the 'Real Life Horse Whisperer', at 7.15am on 30 April 1993 in a petrol station in Chantille, France. Proof indeed of the Zen saying, 'when the student is ready the teacher will appear'.

I could never repay all that Monty Roberts has given to me and his role in helping me on the path to Intelligent Horsemanship. All I can do is try to empower other horsemen and women in the way Monty has empowered me to do the work that I feel is so important. I have also picked up ideas for this book from having worked with some other wonderful horsepeople over the years; that's as well as having to laboriously figure out so much for myself, making plenty of mistakes along the way. I've also witnessed some really horrible horsemanship and some truly evil treatment where I was powerless to help the horses concerned at the time. As a result, this book is my way of giving something back so you don't have to spend thirty plus years of your life working out how to do the best for your horses.

Please forgive me for being rather proud of the work of my students, some of whose own case studies I have included in this book. You will see that in each case Intelligent Horsemanship isn't just about what they do but it is how they think. My aim for my students is that they should go away from a course with a foundation to solve their own 'challenges with horses'. This is also my sincere aim for you after you have read this book. I'd be the last to claim this book has all the answers, but it's certainly a starting point for realising how much information and solutions there are. I honestly believe that if you work through this book methodically and in the spirit it is intended you will have a happier relationship and a happier horse with as Perfect Manners as it is possible for him to achieve. Your only problems will be turning down all those six-figure offers for him.

Kelly Marks

PART I

*the rules of*

TRAINING

# the philosophy of
# PERFECT MANNERS

The word 'manners' can seem rather old fashioned nowadays but I make no apology for praising the presence of them in horses (and indeed humans). Good manners help life along, making all those daily interactions so much less stressful and overall one's life among others more pleasant. Horses that have been taught good manners are often considered more intelligent and sensitive and will have every chance of being treated better in later life, particularly if their future is unknown. With good manners they are less likely to be pushed and pulled around for being 'stupid' or 'ignorant'. Manners are not at all difficult to instil in your horse; all you need to do is gain his or her trust and respect using considerate and consistent techniques. Working on yourself, however, may be more challenging and requires a dedication to studying life from the horse's point of view. Manners may not be everything, but they lay a firm foundation and understanding for all your future interaction.

As with children, horses need educating as to what 'the rules' of good manners are; it's ridiculous to expect horses to know what you want of them. It's no good saying, 'He's just being naughty – he should know he's meant to stand still as I'm brushing his girth!' But how and why should we expect him to know? Also remember manners work both ways. Look at it from the other point of view. Is your horse thinking, 'She knows I hate my girth being brushed that hard'? Remember that, as with humans, so much of what comes naturally to horses turns out to be unacceptable in polite society! A horse that drags you across the yard to investigate a tasty patch of grass, for instance, is performing a very natural act. Why should we expect him to know what is or isn't acceptable? It shouldn't be his job to read our minds, and this is particularly difficult when different people allow different things. The same person expecting different actions at different times is also confusing for the horse. How is he expected to know that normally you consider it sweet and affectionate if he rubs his head all over you any time he wants to, but then you are suddenly furious because he does it when you are all

INNATE UNDERSTANDING
IT ISN'T A HORSE'S JOB TO BE A
MIND READER.

kitted up in your show outfit? The important thing when teaching your horse good manners is that you are prepared to clearly and calmly explain to the horse what you consider good manners to be. Then you need to make sure you try to behave consistently.

## A 'CODE OF CONDUCT'

It really is worth writing out your own 'code of conduct' for your horse, and while you're at it, do one for yourself as well. How would he rate your manners? For example, if your horse agrees to stand still to have his saddle put on, you must agree to place it on his back gently. If the desired mutual manners are established early on in the horse/owner relationship, many of the more serious problems that can develop can be avoided.

Horses learn quickly; they have needed to, in order to survive. They will often learn in just one lesson what to avoid, which for many people has worked to their disadvantage. Horses soon learn that, 'If she gets hold of your ears it hurts', as someone grabs their ears to keep them still for worming, for example, or even if just some well-meaning but clumsy person bends their ears over to push the bridle on. They also quickly learn that if someone is in a hurry with their clipping, and doesn't both-

*Good manners are those which show the greatest sensitivity to others and makes them feel at ease; which avoid all actions which annoy them, force unpleasantness upon them, remove their freedom of choice or make them feel smaller. At the heart of true good manners lies an underlying respect for others and for their rights.*

MODERN ETIQUETTE, MOYRA BREMNER

er to put in the extra oil the clippers clearly need, it will burn them and they won't want to risk that again. However, the good news is, if you first gain their trust, and consistently present clear alternatives, they can learn behavioural patterns that are even contrary to their basic instincts, as well as reverse the ones we label 'problems'.

At no stage are we looking to produce a robotic obedience as in a master/slave relationship, nor do we ever want to produce that sad, blank look you sometimes see in the eyes of animals performing routinely, never having had their feelings considered.

The concepts of good behaviour are nearly always transferable from one situation to another. If your horse isn't doing as you would like, you must accept it as your responsibility. If we are supposedly the 'coach' in the horse/human relationship, then we have to keep thinking, 'How can I go about this in such a way that my horse will understand it is best to do this?'

Remember your horse only has limited ways of communicating to you that he doesn't like something. These include:

- Making faces
- Twitching ears
- Swishing his tail
- Pawing or stamping the ground
- Moving or pulling away.

If he is trapped in a small space this can even escalate into biting or kicking. Communication is a two-way process. If you train yourself to notice and respond to his early communication you will avoid him ever having to feel the need to resort to his own equivalent of 'SHOUTING'.

## THE MEANING OF MANNERS

When I refer to 'manners' in this book, I'm applying the term to horses that 'don't know better'. Generally, they're behaving in an anti-social or difficult way because nobody has ever explained to them that there's a more polite and easier way to interact. A horse that moves off impatiently as you try to get on, is very different from a horse that shoots off in a panic at the prospect of being ridden.

Of course, horse problems can escalate, and it may not take long for a minor issue to develop into a full-scale disaster. It may even be that the approach you use is quite similar, whether dealing with a deep-rooted phobia or a niggling bad habit, and you need to adapt your approach to different problems. None of the exercises in this book should make the situation worse, as long as they are applied correctly. Do be honest with yourself, though, about your level of skill and patience, and if you find yourself dealing with a situation that turns out to be a lot more complicated than you thought, do consider taking on competent, professional help.

You may well find that the solutions and procedures I give in this book both help resolve the particular issue you are dealing with at the time and influence other areas of your interaction as well, which will greatly improve your whole relationship with your horses and, indeed, your whole time together.

Every young horse needs to be introduced to the various expectations that will soon become a part of his everyday life. You will find that good habits established now will stand him in good stead for the rest of

It's a funny thing – the better you get at training, the cleverer your horses become!

*Case study*

# SO MANY PEOPLE WATCH BUT THEY DON'T SEE

*On my first demonstration of the October 2000 tour we were very short of horses to look at in the afternoon so we had no choice but to go for the horse described as a '17hh Stallion: you can't lead him, he bites, he kicks, but the main problem is the rider always needs help getting on because as soon as you go to mount he rears straight up'! He actually turned out to be a smashing big horse. In common with so many of these 'all-in-one' remedials, his main problem was that he was as stiff as a board and had no idea where to put his feet. As well as Join Up and other work, I spent over ten minutes backing him through poles placed in an 'L' shape so he had to go backwards and turn at a right angle.*

*As I started this remedial horse, it did go through my head, 'This is not going to be easy.' The horse was very stiff, clumsy and seemed not to understand what I was asking at all, but over a 15-minute period the minimal improvements were becoming something significant. Suddenly it all 'clicked' for him; he was listening to what I was asking and was yielding and relaxed with the requests. When his rider came to get on, this horse was an angel. He stood absolutely still, with nobody holding him.*

*Afterwards we heard someone being quite dismissive, saying, 'Well, they just picked a really easy horse and she didn't really do anything except tell stories.' Now, I'd love to say it didn't worry me to hear a comment like that, but really I was mortified. I realized, though, that it was my own fault. I've never been impressed with people that ask for a round of applause for doing very little. On the other hand, they've probably learned more quickly than I have that people often don't appreciate things unless they are very clearly pointed out to them. It is tempting to ask the owner to work with the horse first, and then say, 'OK, we'll watch you deal with him for a while to show how difficult he is ...', but that may not be fair on the horses or owners.*

*Make no mistake, I could get a horse to behave badly if I wanted to (and so could anyone). I think some people almost subsciously do this to horses in an attempt to impress people with 'heroic' horse handling. By using uncomfortable body language, attitude and rope pressure, in less than a minute you can have a horse that wouldn't allow you to pick up his hind legs, who would rear when you asked him to go forwards, and would be impossible to catch if you let him go. Please be clear on this point as well. If you want to fight a horse, he'll fight you right back ... even though it isn't what he really wants to do at all. This will happen with people as well. If you go up to someone with all guns blazing, accusatory, demanding, you will quickly find yourself in an argument and neither of you even knows what it is about. If this has been your tendency in the past, you have an opportunity now to make a choice. You can carry on in the same way or you can make a decision to 'take a breath' in future and think things through intelligently before acting. As always, the choice is yours.*

*When I am demonstrating, I make sure I explain to the audience how I'm working to avoid con-frontation as far as I can. People need to watch with the right pair of eyes. Please read this book with the right eyes as well. Understand that everything is built up from the foundation. Sometimes an extra brick added here and there doesn't look very much. However, if you keep working in the right way, in time you can really achieve something substantial and beautiful.*

his life. It is always better to prevent a problem rather than having to work later on the much harder job of trying to cure one. Don't be despondent if you are working with an older horse; these methods are tried and tested and have worked on horses who are in their teens or even twenties!

## UNDERSTANDING THE CONCEPTS

This is not a 'quick fixes for your horse' book. While I have seen books that suggest 'if your horse does that, you just do this', there is a danger they only paper over the cracks in such a way that doesn't do any justice to the horse or handler in the long term. In my experience many of the problems, large and small, I've come up against with horses is largely due to the fact that the horse was never taught any differently in the first place. Sometimes it was because the horse was always found difficult that things were glossed over in his initial training. Sometimes it's because the horse was always so delightfully easy that some little inconveniences were overlooked.

I've designed this book so you can first of all understand the philosophy and concepts as a whole. Then you should work through the Foundation Exercises (see pages 58-73), making sure no part of the groundwork training has been left out. When you have completed the exercises, jot the results down in a notebook. There is also a section on Join Up (see pages 86-107), which is a powerful method of communicating with your horse devised by Monty Roberts to create a strong bond with your horse. In the second half of the book I look at specific problems, although once you have done the preliminary exercises these may become irrelevant.

## HORSES FOR COURSES

Some people think there are two types of people in this world: those that think there are two types of people in the world; and those that think this is utter rubbish. Personally I don't think there is, and I don't believe there are two types of horses either. It would make my life so much easier if there were, as I could say, 'Listen, you either do this, or you do this.' So simple. Of course, there are plenty of things that are true for a majority of horses. There are many similarities among horses and I really hope the advice I give will work in different circumstances for most horses around the world. It's always your duty, though, to evaluate what is going on with a particular horse at a particular time. Always try to read what the horse is doing and saying, not what he should be doing. I'm giving the best advice I can, but remember, I'm sitting by a computer, typing and drinking tea. You're the one with the horse – and you're the only one that really knows what's going on right now.

I have been lucky enough to work with many different breeds of

horses throughout my life from shires and cobs to thoroughbreds, Arabs and hackneys. Hackneys are one of the most sensitive breeds I have ever come across, and this has probably led to them being greatly misunderstood in the past. When I run a course it is one of my responsibilities to try and match people to horses to the best of my ability (it's when people want to take the horse home with them that I know I've done too good a job!). Later on in the course students are ready to adapt to a variety of different horses but, depending on their personality, there are generally certain types of horses that are more compatible with their personality than others. For example, if you are a weekend rider who just wants to have a safe hack out from time to time, a kind-natured cob that lives outside is probably going to be perfect for you. However, if you want to be an international showjumper, clearly the horse just mentioned is going to be a source of frustration and disappointment. Such matching of horse with rider must always be borne in mind. Sometimes 'the horses with problems' that people contact me about are actually quite perfect – but for somebody else.

I see far more people 'over horsed' than the other way round. It's an injustice for the horse and a source of unhappiness for the humans when people buy a horse that clearly has needs and potential far beyond them. Looking at any problems you may have, I would ask you, first of all, to be realistic in what it is you really need from your horse and what you can offer him in return.

## PREPARATION

Some of you may want your horse to have perfect manners to assist you when competing in the show ring. To achieve success in competition, if that is what you really want, requires focus, determination and preparation – the qualities that will help you win (talent helps but is by no means obligatory). Be aware that 'winners don't leave things up to luck'. Could you imagine, for example, top show producers getting ready for the *Horse of the Year Show*, saying, 'Gosh, I do hope our horses won't be put off by the big crowds indoors. Oh well, we'd better keep our fingers crossed'.?

What happens in real life is that professionals in these circumstances never leave things to chance. All the horses and their riders are taken to a convenient indoor school, which provides a great sound system. Friends, relations, children and dogs are brought along and positively encouraged to behave incredibly badly. They run up and down the galleries, lean over the edges waving flags, shout and jump around, and once the horses learn to be unfazed by this, then the BBC soundtrack of loud cheering, noisy aeroplanes, big bands, blazing fireworks and cannon fire comes on. As the saying goes, 'the harder you work the luckier you get'.

> An amateur will practise until they can get it right.
> A professional will practise until they can't get it wrong.

**THE BRIGHTER SIDE OF LIFE**
SOME HORSES ARE SO DELIGHTFULLY EASY THAT LITTLE INCONVENIENCES GET OVERLOOKED.

# *a zebra in*
# YOUR STABLE?

Perhaps genetic alteration has taken us a fair way from the 'zebra in our stable' and I'm not necessarily a believer in 'natural is always best.' In Joel Berger's *Horses of the Great Basin* there is a photograph of three beautiful wild mares on the front cover, and you read later in the book that they all died that winter in a snow storm. Nature can be very hard. It's popular to talk about having your horse as a 'partner' and yet the same people who speak that way put him in an environment over which he has very little control and expect to dictate most of his moves. It's therefore worth studying and appreciating the true nature of horses, so you can relate to them and understand life more from their point of view. Take any opportunity to study horses in natural herds or even just a few horses out in the field together. Look through the following points of interest in relation to horses kept naturally – see if it could have any bearing on your own homegrown 'zebra'.

## HORSES LIVE IN GROUPS

Horses are used to living in groups – called 'herds' or, more scientifically, 'bands'. Although mustangs and other types are often referred to as 'wild' they are really 'feral', i.e. their ancestors were once domesticated. The only truly wild horses are Przewalski's horses. Horses are naturally gregarious creatures, so if another horse isn't available they will pair up with another creature and this, of course, includes humans.

A typical family group consists of a stallion, who is mainly in the 'driving' position, keeping everyone together, mating with mares and looking out for threats from other stallions. There may be a couple of mares, or as many as 12 with foals, yearlings and others that haven't started breeding. There is usually one dominant mare who decides where the group goes. Once the youngsters get old enough to breed they are pushed into bachelor herds or into other 'harems'.

Although in wildlife television programmes you see horses spending a lot of time mating and having spectacular fights, this has more to do

CONTENTMENT IS ... 'REAL LIFE' HAS LESS TO DO WITH SEX AND VIOLENCE AND MORE TO DO WITH EATING.

with humans preferring to watch sex and violence than to watching them peacefully eating. (Although with the popularity of so many cooking programmes nowadays maybe this is debatable.) The main interest of horses in the wild is to survive and reproduce, and up to 70 per cent of their time is spent grazing. All members of the band will indulge in mutual grooming, which they use to establish friendship. Tactile stimulation is clearly important to the horse. A horse can feel a fly on his skin and twitch it off but many humans treat horses in too heavy-handed a manner. Every horse handler needs to appreciate a horse's sensitivity and enjoyment of touch and also the relationship between physiology and psychology with regard to the horse. Young horses particularly will be seen to 'play' and if we can get them to think of our educating them as fun, we're going to have a happier and more willing horse.

## WILD HORSES

To optimize training, proper management of the horse's life and environment is essential. All of us so enjoy seeing a horse looking well, but can get side-tracked as to what 'looking well' really is. If you have to have a horse wearing a duvet and a rug all through the summer months (believe me, people do this), not allowing him any time in the field, and if he's also obese, you can't honestly claim that you really know the meaning of 'looking well'. Well meaning is not the same as well being for the horse. Of course, if show-ring glory is your ultimate aim, you may feel the need to take this route, and some horses will adapt to this routine better than others. However, the average riding horse is better off with a more natural life style, being turned out at least every day, if not full time, and fed in proportion to the amount of work he's doing. A great deal of the problems I hear about could be avoided if the horses were fed and exercised appropriately.

## AN ANIMAL THAT FLEES

The horse is a flight animal not a fight animal ...
Being a prey animal rather than a predator, i.e. you're the dinner, not the diner, gives you a very different perspective on life. A horse's natural instinct is to take flight – run first and ask questions later. Perhaps females can understand the horse's perspective of feeling vulnerable better than males: to be walking down a street alone late at night; to be the only person in a train carriage and a lone male steps in; your car breaks down on a lonely country road. How we feel and react, of course, will depend to some degree on our history and how we've been brought up to react in these cases. It's the same with horses; it's not reasonable to expect a horse never to be frightened, but you need to do everything in your power to build his trust in you. By gaining his respect and focus, you may ask that even when he is frightened he behaves in a controlled

fashion. Remember also – every time you cause the flight animal pain, you are giving him every right to fear you.

## BODY MOVEMENTS

Horses use a lot of body movement and posturing to communicate ...
Rather than expect them to be able to read our minds, we need to learn horses' language as much as possible. While not suggesting everything they do is a specific communication to us or each other, still a swishing of the tail can be clearly read as indicating irritation or a yawn usually indicates a release of stress, or better still letting go of it completely. Get to know your horse personally and learn to 'read' what he could be saying; observe if there's always a certain time when he performs particular actions. From his observation of herd behaviour, the Californian horse trainer Monty Roberts, known to many as 'the real-life horse whisperer', explained to me that when a youngster is misbehaving, one of the older mares will discipline him. She does this by pushing him out of the herd and not letting him back in until he has exhibited sufficient 'apologetic' behaviour, i.e. licking and chewing and lowering his head.

A horse will prove his dominance by being able to impel another horse to move around. While some behaviourists and ethologists are almost obsessive about the 'dominance hierarchies' and 'pecking orders' (an idea that arose from work in Germany [Schjelderup-Ebbe 1913] on chickens) that might exist among horses, others feel this is less an issue in 'real life' where horses aren't often competing for small amounts of food, which is when these issues mainly arise

Concentrating only on dominance doesn't give a balanced view. Certainly some horses will dominate others, but it is important that we also appreciate the horse's desire to bond and form friendships and understand that the horse's most natural wish is to live in co-operation rather than conflict. If you offer horses two options, an easy one and a more difficult one, providing they understand they will take the path of least resistance – it's true to their nature. In the herd, horses are quickly influenced by the emotions and actions of others – this is often known as the 'herd instinct'. For example, if one respected horse in the herd suddenly lifts its head to look at something in the distance, all the others will look up immediately. When the first horse realizes that there isn't a problem and goes back to eating, all the others will follow suit. Be aware of this when you think how your emotions and actions may affect your horse.

> The horse's most natural wish is to live in co-operation rather than conflict.

## LEARNING ABILITY

Horses learn quickly and 'unlearn' slowly ...
Prey animals have to be quick learners. If a predator makes a mistake he doesn't get any dinner that night; if a prey animal makes a mistake he

becomes dinner that night. It's also important that they learn quickly what isn't harmful, otherwise all prey animals would spend their whole time running away and never have time to rest, eat and reproduce. Horses can be trained to ignore things that frighten the average human, if they are educated correctly. Just think, for example, of how police and cavalry horses face up to danger.

## THE BRAIN

There seems to be a saying bandied around that 'the horse has a brain the size of a walnut'. It's both untrue and disrespectful ...

To suggest that if someone is willing to generously work for you they must be stupid speaks more of you as an employer than it does of the employee. Everyone's 'intelligence' varies anyway. The size of one's brain is by no means the ultimate guide to intelligence. There are many factors, such as the brains size in relation to the animal's body and indeed to how it is used. The average horse's brain weighs about 650g (23oz) – a very large walnut – and the front part is in overlapping layers. The outside layer (the neocortex) deals with thinking, imagining, planning and talking. The neocortex of the human brain is over twice the size (relatively speaking) of the horse. It is now generally accepted that the inner layer (limbic system) deals with feelings and emotional reactions (pain and pleasure) and is also the seat of learning. Relatively speaking, it is around the same size in horses and humans, which may give added credibility to the claim that horses are emotional creatures if, indeed, we ever doubted it.

## THE SENSES

You must take into account all the horse's senses – eyesight, hearing, touch, taste and smell ...

The horse is very perceptive in all his senses: they are essential for him to survive in the wild. This could explain why his senses are often more acute than ours, and why he reacts far more quickly than we do. With so much sensory stimulation most human beings have learned to switch off to a great deal of what is going on around them. Something I have found fun when out riding is, when my horse suddenly sees, hears or smells something, trying to discover what it is he's noticed. It's fascinating – you find out how much you've been missing over the years!

As a horse's sense of smell is so particularly aucte, be aware that the perfume you wear may be very nice to other human beings but repellent or confusing to your horse. Indeed, horses can smell fear or anger in a human by recognizing the pheromones we emit. It has been demonstrated that on a windy day your horse is not just being 'silly' if he plays up; the wind is actually stopping him hearing properly and it can be worrying and confusing to him.

**I CAN SEE YOU**
KEEP TRYING TO UNDERSTAND
LIFE FROM THE HORSE'S POINT
OF VIEW.

## THE HORSE'S PERSPECTIVE

Horses see life (and everything else) very differently from how we do ...
To see in the same way as a horse we need a horse's brain but it is
important that we at least try to understand this fundamental difference between horse and human. How we see the world to a large extent
explains how we make many of our judgements and organize our thinking. The horse is a typical prey animal: its eyes are positioned on the side
of its head and have a huge peripheral field of vision – 340 degrees of
the 360 degrees around it. Our eyes are placed in front of our head, as
they are in other 'hunters' such as cats or dogs. We have excellent depth
perception and can judge distances easily. A horse can find this far more
difficult and it may explain why he is reluctant to step into a puddle at
first, as he doesn't know if it's a few inches deep or bottomless. Also:

- He has the largest eyes of any land mammal.
- He has two narrow blind spots – one immediately behind him and
  the other up to 2m (6ft) in front of him and beneath his nose.
  (Maybe not completely blind – just goes out of focus.)
- He has excellent long-distance vision, raising his head for this.
- To see where he is putting his front feet he has to lower his head.
- He has an incredible ability to discern movement.
- He has binocular vision in the middle.
- Glaring white catches his eye very well, which is why it's a good
  colour for stud fences.

> I'll give you the best advice
> I can but you are the one with
> your horse. Listen to your horse.
> Listen to yourself.

*Case study*

# STARTING A WILD HORSE IN ARGENTINA

*After completing my Preliminary Certificate course with Kelly in Oxfordshire, I went to Argentina to spend as much time with horses as I could and ended up staying a whole year. I learned so much with so many different horses. One young mare in particular, Ginger, taught me a lesson that would probably be unusual to experience while working with a horse in the UK.*

*Ginger was three years old, and had had the traditional upbringing of having no contact with humans before me, although she lived with a herd of tame horses that were used by gauchos. Several times a day, I began to work at getting near her as she dodged me in a small pen. By changing my aggressive/inviting body language, communication was soon established. As time went on and it came to leading her, for some sessions she walked straight into the pen and progressed very well, but at other times she was less than keen to go into the pen and would become annoyed and uncommunicative within a few minutes. I found it impossible to predict these quite distinct moods.*

*I did notice, however, that she had a real aversion to the metal clip on the long line I used; she flinched at the feel of the metal and the small metallic sound of the clip being put on the headcollar, which took her by surprise every time. I progressed at a pace I felt was right for her and had a bridle and saddle on her within a week or so. Both myself and the gaucho who helped me were surprised when she didn't seem disturbed by the saddle and made no attempt to buck. However, when I first leant over her she suddenly went mad. When I came round (thank heavens for my Charles Owen hat that it wasn't worse) I was able to analyse what had happened. It was a sound that had frightened her – the sound of the stirrup touching something metallic as I leant over had sent her into a frenzy.*

*The biggest lesson Ginger taught me was that you need to account for all the horses' senses, particularly when starting youngsters. Hearing is the sense that horses are most sensitive to, but this is not something that most horses need to be de-sensitized to, unless, like Ginger, they live in the middle of nowhere and have been brought up on a vast open plain. The world of most horses born wild in Argentina is virtually silent: in most of the UK, 'noise pollution' accustoms horses to sudden sounds without us realizing it. I should have realized, by reading Ginger's reactions, that because of her quiet life thus far, metallic sounds must have been particularly alien to her – as she had been indicating to me all along. The smallest metallic noise had made a huge and frightening impact on her, as it has now made a huge impact on me. In spite of this early traumatic experience, however, she is now, I've heard from her owners, a lovely ride, and a pleasure to own.*

**INTELLIGENT HORSEMANSHIP RECOMMENDED ASSOCIATE DIANA MACLEAN**

• He is unable to pick out fine detail but can make out silhouettes.

• He has excellent night vision (at least in comparison to humans). Horses need to learn to see things from both sides. Each eye of a horse works separately, which could explain why it seems we must teach a horse to look at everything on the ground from both sides. Compared to the way the human brain works, the horse has only a limited ability to cross-refer between the right and left hemispheres of the cerebral cortex. If all the work with him has been done from one side only (usually the nearside), he may then react in surprise when approached from the off side. When the rider is mounted for the first time, one should be careful when bending the horse's head to the offside for the first time, even though the horse has seen the rider from the other, nearside eye. If a horse is good to handle on the nearside but not on the off, it is often because he has only been handled on that side. However, if a horse is frightened on the nearside but doesn't mind you on the offside, there is a high possibility that he has been roughly handled or hit on the nearside but left alone on the offside. Most horses are 'left-handed', preferring to run to the left than the right, so it could be that the horse is trying to keep that flight option free.

## GOOD HABITS

The horse can easily become a creature of habit ...

Even in the wild, the more a horse does something 'well', meaning he received some sort of reward for it and was not punished, the more likely he is to do the same thing the next time. The seeking of pleasure and avoidance of pain is inherent in all of us. As he is a creature who prefers to take the path of least resistance, he is very likely to establish habits easily as it makes his life so much better. Encourage this tendency, to work for you, rather than against you. Establish good habits from the start. To help avoid problems, if, say, you do flat work in the same area regularly, don't always stop in the same place or soon he will be slowing up every time he comes to that area. If you always get off in the middle of the school, soon he'll be hankering to get to the middle.

> Make every effort to establish good habits right from the start.

The more a horse does something in certain circumstances the more likely he is to do it again in the same circumstances. It even sets up entirely different neurological pathways in the brain that become more efficient with every repetition. But just as repetition is the backbone of building habits so prevention of repetition is a necessary part of breaking the unwanted habits. Supposing, for instance, a horse always shied, napped or refused at a certain point, you can break the pattern just by something as simple as reversing past the object. Sometimes you can foresee a negative pattern starting up; for example, when you plait your horse he realizes that he's going to a show and leaves his feed. If this is the case, change his routine to avoid any anxiety starting.

# *the rules of* TRAINING

When you start your initial training always work in an enclosed area with a soft, non-slip surface. An ideal area for doing the initial training exercises would be about 15–18m (50–60ft) across, and round or square pens are better than oblong. Your life with horses can be made much easier if they never get to realize how much stronger they are than us. One of the ways of ensuring this is by always working in an enclosed area until you are quite sure they are safe and understand the benefits of staying with you. If a youngster or remedial horse does get loose in an enclosure, it doesn't matter at all – you simply pick up the rope or long line again, and the horse is usually unaware that anything has even happened. In the United States and Australia many accidents are avoided because round pens and 'yards' are normal for the initial handling, leading and riding of young horses. More and more people are appreciating the benefits of using these in Britain, the most important aspect being the safety of horse and handler. If you are handling horses you don't know from the ground, always make sure that you have an escape route, in case there is trouble of any kind. Ideally, have other people who are near enough to contact, who are willing to check in on you from time to time to make sure everything is going well.

Protect your horse in every way you can, and also protect yourself. Wear a hard hat and good boots – I like to wear gloves because that means that I can work with horses all day but don't have to eat dinner with red, raw hands covered in blisters. It's absolutely not the case that gloves give you insensitive hands when riding; look at any of the top competition riders. 'Hands' are just as much about your independent seat than your fingers, but obviously gloves need to be very lightweight so that any sensitivity lost is negligible.

With some problems you may be tempted to think that if you could get your horse in a really small area, he will be much easier to handle because then 'he can't get away'. The trouble with this way of thinking is that if the horse is being difficult because he is frightened, and then

A HORSE IS A JOY

'A PONY IS A CHILDHOOD DREAM. A HORSE IS AN ADULT TREASURE.' REBECCA CARROLL feels 'trapped' in a small area, it can make him think he has to fight for his life – and this is when people and horses can get hurt. Just think about any leg handling or clipping problem you know. I'd like to bet that the handlers are (not unreasonably) trying to deal with the problem in the stable. Has the fact that the horse hasn't much room to manoeuvre cured the problem? Very unlikely. Although some handling work can be made easier by holding a horse in a very small space – when vets examine mares, for instance – to change a horse's attitude we want him to make the choice that it's more comfortable to be with us. That's what is going to make the difference.

## ONE STEP AT A TIME

If an aspect of your training isn't working, especially if you find your horse or yourself getting frustrated, it's nearly always best to take a step back for a while to find out where the misunderstandings lie. As with all problems, rather than regard it as one enormous, insurmountable task, it's best to break things down into manageable chunks. I often find it helpful to write things down as this enables me look at the situation more clearly.

## PROBLEM SOLVING

First of all define what the problem actually is. I have many calls about horses with problems. A person may say, 'I can't get a bridle on my horse.' If the last horse I dealt with was, say, ear shy, it's tempting to immediately start telling the person how to proceed with an ear-shy horse. What we've got to do first, though, is actually define the problem. Why can't she get the bridle on the horse? Is it because he won't let his ears be touched? Is it because he puts his head too high? Is it because he won't open his mouth? Or perhaps it's because he's in a large field and she can't catch him!

Once you've defined the problem you can try to work out the cause. It's good to know the origin of the problem just in case you can prevent the same thing happening again. However, sometimes all you can really do is make your best guess and proceed methodically to help the horse, whatever the cause. It can often be related to ignorance or welfare issues at previous homes. You can

> A horse isn't aware of his own strength other than that shown by his experience.

**FRIGHTENED OF PIGS**
**SHOW YOUR HORSE THERE IS**
**NOTHING TO FEAR.**

learn a great deal about a horse's past from his signs and reactions, but the fact is, we often never really know the whole story and we can only do our effort to apologise on behalf of the human race, and reassure the horse as best we can in order to gain his trust and respect.

Incidentally, if you need to ring me or one of the Intelligent Horsemanship Recommended Associates about a horse with problems, it's always best if you can give us the symptom first. So often I get people on the phone and they start by describing the horses' grandparents and where they bought him and why they wanted a horse in the first place. Once I know the symptom, then I have far more idea of what's relevant in his past, and I will be able to ask specific questions to piece the puzzle together.

## REGRESSION IN TRAINING

Training doesn't always proceed in a linear fashion. Animal trainers have found that there are sometimes cases where an animal appears to be going backwards in his training for a period of time before it gets better. In some cases this can be connected with latent learning.

There's a saying that goes: 'If your only tool is a hammer then every problem will be a nail'. Watch out for this. Beware if all your solutions for the horses you deal with seem to go in runs. You hear of people whose advice for every horse problem is some piece of equipment. Another person will find physical difficulties with every single horse. Even if you have got a vast array of 'tools', be aware that sometimes you can still have the last horse you dealt with on your mind and it's comfortable to find the same 'slot' for the next horse. It's interesting how farriers will say (and genuinely believe) that 90 per cent of horses' problems stem from something wrong with their feet, while saddle fitters will say 90 per cent of horses' problems come from a badly fitting saddle. Guess what equine dental technicians say? It's human nature that if something succeeds, or it is our area of expertise, we will naturally turn towards trying the same solution again next time.

In my experience of people telling me what they've already tried for 'curing' any problem, the top three seem to be 'hit him', 'lunge him' or 'turn him out for a year'. I am not saying these things can never work,

## THE APPLIANCE OF SCIENCE

Just in case you are feeling there's too much homespun wisdom in this book, it's time for the appliance of science.

1 The 'law of requisite variety' says: *'In any system, human or machine, all other things being equal, the widest range of potential responses can control the system'*. This means flexibility in your thinking is what's going to get you ahead. Does your horse have seven different ways of evading you? It means you only need to have eight different answers to stay ahead.

2 *'For every action there is an equal and opposite reaction.'* This means if you go to fight your horse, you can be sure he'll fight you right back. But you love to meet things head on? BECOME A BOXER!

FEARLESS NOW ... (OVERLEAF)
IF A HORSE IS FRIGHTENED WE HAVE TO HELP HIM OVERCOME THAT FEAR.

*Case study*

# SAFFRON, THE BICYCLE-PHOBIC PONY

I've worked with some delightful horses and ponies (and donkeys) because of the BBC 1 'Barking Mad!' programmes and 'Saffron, the Bicycle-Phobic Pony' was no exception. When I first saw this lovely, unstarted, three-year-old Welsh pony and heard about his 'phobia' with bicycles, I was inclined to think that it must be a general nervousness because of his inexperience. However, as I got to know a little more about him, I found a pony who happily accepted cars and ten-ton trucks speeding past him but if he saw a bicycle over 100 yards away on the road down below, he would run around his stable, snorting, kicking and breaking out in a sweat. Needless to say, if his owner was leading him out and a bicycle came in the vicinity, Saffron soon broke away and ran off.

The handler at this stage was Kerry Dibble, a kind and capable horse handler but baffled by Saffron's behaviour. Saffron was eventually intended for Kristen, his nine-year-old daughter, but at the time was too dangerous for her to lead, let alone think of riding. I watched Saffron, Kerry and the bikes on my first visit, realized the problem was serious, and starting working out a plan that I hope may be helpful to readers as well. Much of this plan can be adapted to work with different types of phobias or fears.

Saffron turned out to be the most delightful pony to have around: very huggable and affectionate and only worried about those dreaded bicycles. He joined up very strongly in the round pen from day one and we even carried on slowly during the week, preparing for me to be his first rider. He didn't need more than three Join Ups as he became very bonded to the person in the pen, following them around closely and comfortably. It was then I wondered what would happen if I had a bicycle in the

*pen with me. I went in the round pen pushing a bike and Saffron immediately did his familiar 'bike snort' and trotted off around the outside. I slowly wheeled the bike after him. As Saffron was already familiar with the process and I was actually wheeling round very passively, my eyes down, Saffron soon looked in to assess the situation. As soon as he looked at the bike and me, I wheeled the bike away from him by a couple of yards. This is known as advance and retreat, a method that has worked with prey animals since time began. Any prey animal knows that a predator intent on killing doesn't move away once a victim is in their sights. This approach gave Saffron confidence to come forward and feel unthreatened. I waited a moment and then started to move the bike slowly around the back of him again. But Saffron slowly turned with me, and started following the bike. After a complete circuit I stopped and gave him a lovely rub. I then moved off in the other direction and he followed more confidently behind. I asked the students to give him a gentle round of applause. I thought, 'Maybe we could have something for the television programme after all'. Saffron was completely unfazed by the applause, simply taking it as his due, as gradually it got louder, with whoops and cheers.*

*Saffron behaved admirably on his final day of filming for the BBC. I was very proud of him and as usual it was a combination of the work done rather than just one thing. The advance and retreat work in the round pen with the bike had a great deal to do with building up his confidence. It allowed him to feel more in control. He realized that he could keep the bike safely in his sights by simply following round after it rather than running away. I did smile when Kerry was filming on the final day. The first time Saffron saw a bike on this occasion he gently started to follow it – much to Kerry's amazement!*

just that the repertoire needs dramatically extending. Why do people limit themselves in this way? Let me divulge the secret: I believe it's because it's something they know how to do. Most of us feel most comfortable doing the things with which we are most familiar. Let us, as more progressive horse people, expand our thinking and look at other possibilities that might bring the results we are searching for.

While I encourage all my students to make a 'check list' of possible problems and solutions with any new horse they come across, even with this fairly comprehensive 'tool kit', you can still get stuck in a rut and it's the worst idea to stifle imagination in people. How will we ever make great new discoveries if we only ever stick to a set of very narrow ideas that we are already sure about? I am very pleased to be able to include case studies of my students as well as my own so you can see that while 'plan A' may have been carried out to perfection, if that didn't bring about the desired results we may have to go on to plan b, c or d. This stops one getting stuck in a plan and can also produce that little extra flair which makes all the difference between 'OK' and something remarkable being achieved. You might never know exactly the next step you are going to take with a horse; all you do know is that you are going to keep things as safe as you possibly can, as calm as you possibly can, and you are going to make that horse trust you and want to work with you, not to fear you.

A section of the weekend 'Horse Psychology' courses that I run are dedicated to possible ways of approaching problems; not just running through a check list but using some imagination as well.

### GOOD QUESTIONS TO ASK WHEN PROBLEMS OCCUR
• What is my horse saying, or what is he thinking now?
Try to get inside the horse's mind. It's no good asking a horse to talk if you're not listening. Instead, study the horse's senses and the way his mind works.

• What would be the craziest solution you could come up with?
Have a brainstorming session over the problem. There's nothing like having good friends to discuss problems with; they don't even have to be knowledgeable about horses. In fact, it's often an advantage if they're not. I don't mean you have to do the crazy thing, but get thinking, use your imagination; it might just spark off something sensible – you never know.

• If you wanted to create this problem how would you do it? (Then think of the opposite.)
Yes, I know that this seems weird but it's what Edward do Bono (who's made an art of studying problem solving) calls 'upside-down thinking'.

> Remember, just because something is your idea and you didn't read it in a book first or were told it by some expert, doesn't meant it's not brilliant.

Sometimes it can really give you a new insight into a predicament. For instance, if I wanted to teach a horse how to bolt, how would I do it? I'd overfeed and under-exercise him (always a good start). I'd make sure his mouth got gradually desensitized by continuous rough handling at every pace. I'd always gallop on the same stretch of ground (preferably towards home), gradually allowing the horse to start off earlier and earlier as he begins to anticipate what's to come.

One could incorporate bolting 'for joy' with this system, but if you insist on introducing fear, then for best results, pain would have to be brought into the picture, possibly with a whip but less overtly with a suitably uncomfortable saddle and bad riding. In fact, if the rider is really talented they can bounce around on the horse's back accurately mimicking the movements of an aggressive animal on the horse's most vulnerable areas. A bizarre idea to think about, making your horse bolt? Yes. But does it give you any other ideas that might help you realize how a horse becomes like this in the first place, or how you may help to get over it in the future?

• What is the simplest solution to this problem? (And indeed how important is it really, that this problem is solved?)
Horses can often be quite delightful, but their owners tend to focus on the one area where they are not quite perfect. It may be that this can be improved, but do just think things through. Do the risk/cost analysis as suggested in 'Tying Your Horse' (see page 121). A friend once told me about an 18-year-old horse a person she knew had bought that was known to be terrified of cows. The new owner decided to start to desensitize him to cows in what I thought wasn't an overly ambitious way. She had an old cow hide, which she hung over a door several stables away from him. After she realized the horse was still shaking and hadn't touched his food or water for four days, she decided that 'at this age I think we'll just make sure that he avoids cows in the future.'

> **TRUE STORY**
> One of my students has since told me a heartening 'fear of cows' success story. Her horse was terrified of cows so they put a calf in the stable next door to their horse. After his initial fear subsided he became really happy and comfortable with that particular cow. Unfortunately, though, he is still terrified of every other cow he meets!

I'm not suggesting that you take a defeatist attitude (although personally I would never have held out for that long), but you do need to take into account the horse's age and circumstances, and whether 'curing him' is really for the benefit of the horse or more to do with your ego. In a case like this, I think perhaps the horse was 'imprinted' with this fear very early on in his life and it was too deeply ingrained into his survival system to change.

There is an excellent book out called *Life Strategies*, written by Dr Phil McGraw, who helped Oprah Winfrey win her major court case against the Texas cattle farmers. One chapter is called 'Life Is Not Cured – It's Managed'. This rings particularly true with stable vices but can apply to other undesirable practices as well. You have to do a cost analysis on whether a problem is worth trying to solve or not. Do try to make an intelligent decision as to whether it would it be better to just try and 'manage' the situation.

You can also emulate the self-help gurus and eliminate from your vocabulary the word 'problems' and replace it with 'challenges'. If it helps you approach matters with a more positive attitude then it can only be for the good. For this, you need focus, creativity and sometimes courage when faced with seemingly hopeless cases. Things won't always go perfectly easily and smoothly when dealing with horses. But, as in real life, it's how you cope with failure (or seeming failure) that really shows if you've got what it takes for success. Don't think about the set-backs, but try to remain focused on where you are trying to go with a particular horse. If you can stay calm and focused you won't block off your creativity. As long as you want to work with horses you are going to need to use your brains and imagination – so get used to doing so right from the start.

### ONGOING TRAINING

Remember, all the time you are with your horse you are training him whether you mean to be or not, right from your first greeting in the morning. If you walk across the field to catch another horse and your horse ducks behind a tree, go and give your horse a stroke first before walking on – or he may just think he's found a new clever way of avoiding you. Keep looking at the results you are getting and try to work out 'How have I trained him to do that?' and 'Am I training him to do what I want him to do or what I don't want him to do?'

### VET CHECK

I can't emphasize enough how important it is to make sure that your horse's problems aren't pain-related. It is so often the case, and many times they have no other way of telling us that they are uncomfortable, other than by bucking, shaking their head or refusing to go forward. Also if a horse isn't comfortable it may be he can't actually physically clear a jump or do a lateral move or whatever it is you are asking. The proper starting point for all these issues is to get a good and caring horse vet to come and examine your horse. The vet needs to see him trot up, feel over him, take a look at his teeth, and if the horse seems 'depressed' in any way, may want to take a blood test. Your vet may then go on to recommend a suitable therapist for further work with your horse, i.e. physiotherapist, chiropractor or maybe an osteopath. Remember, vets aren't gods, and never be frightened to question things or get a second opinion. When choosing a vet or alternative practitioner, try to get a personal recommendation and be sure that you have a person that's really right for you and your horse. After all, your horse has to rely on you for this.

Learn as much as you can about how your horse's body works so you are quick to notice if his movements or responses aren't quite normal. Be aware, too, that the horse has reflex points on his body. These evoke natural automatic reactions. In other words, the horse often can't help his reaction when there is pressure in these areas. Some of the reflex points are:

• Just over the loins where predators would jump up and hang on. This is an area where an ill-fitting saddle or bad rider could inadvertently put pressure. In response to this, the horse's reflex action will be to hollow or round his back to get the 'predator' off. In some cases this can result in the horse bucking. In other cases it can merely mean the horse raises his head to adjust to the discomfort. This is a time when the non-sympathetic horseperson can start fitting draw reins or equipment to pull the horse's head down.

• Another reflex point is by the poll, where predators might try and break the horse's neck. Again, badly fitting gadgets or an over tight brow band could result in the horse lifting or shaking his head.

• The underside of the belly is another reflex point, as this is where predators might rip through the skin to get at the stomach and intestines. If a girth or strap goes back there it can trigger the reflex for kicking and bucking. Rodeo horses are fitted with a strap that goes under the 'stifle' area in order to produce this effect.

## TRAINING HALTERS

Conventionally, strong or 'difficult' horses have been led on their bridles. It's not uncommon to see a horse that is being led getting three or four strong jags in the mouth for putting a foot wrong. With the tongue and mouth area being the most vulnerable part of the horse, and yet an area where damage won't be seen if you're not looking for it, I always prefer to work with a training halter than a bridle. Of course, a normal halter is fine for most horses and any equipment has to be used correctly, but I have found training halters invaluable in certain cases.

There are several different types of training halters available on the market. A good training halter can make it much easier for the horse to distinguish your 'Yes' from your 'No' and for setting up an easy line of

> All the time you are with your horse you are training him – whether you mean to be or not.

communication between you and your horse. Also I'm the first to admit that I'm not particularly strong and one of these halters can just give me that bit of extra control when I need it. It's important that we understand that the results we get are not only about equipment; the most important thing is how that equipment is used. Many years ago I first read Olympic gold medallist Bill Steinkraus's book *Riding and Jumping*, and agreed with his comment that 'a bad workman blames his tools, but have you noticed how the best workmen always have the best tools?' Having said that, it's no good having wonderful equipment if you don't know how to use it. But, on the other hand, if you are intending to do a job properly, having just the right equipment to hand can often make all the difference. A training halter should be just that – for training. The measure of how successful your training is will be that you won't need to use the halter except to occasionally remind the horse what you expect of him.

One of the mildest training halters you can work with is the Dually (pronounced 'Dooley') halter. The Dually was designed by Monty Roberts and was given its name by one of our students, Leigh Wills, who is now teaching in New Zealand. As well as being the name of one of Monty's favourite horses, it is particularly apt because it is dual-purpose, having one ring for leading and one for tying up safely. It is just like a normal headcollar but with an extra strap that goes across the front of the nose. It has to be fixed high up on the nose and must not be used lower down on the soft part as that area is particularly sensitive in a horse. It comes in three sizes – small, medium and large – and each can be used on a wider range of head sizes. It is a very useful halter to have in any yard and has the added bonus of being very easy to switch from normal use to schooling use with the result that the horse doesn't get to know when it is easier to take advantage.

**THE DUALLY HALTER**

THE DUALLY HALTER HAS TWO RINGS SO IT CAN BE USED AS A TRAINING HALTER OR A NORMAL HALTER.

It is quite possible to tie a rope in a variety of configurations with or without a headcollar, so do learn to tie one yourself to be ready in an emergency. There are various arrangements you can use that work on similar lines. Some, though – for instance, the war bridle, which Monty Roberts calls the 'comealong', can exert strong pressure particularly over the poll area – can be severe and cause dramatic reactions, such as rearing over backwards. It is definitely not recommended for anyone but expert handlers.

Before you start work always check that the halter fits correctly with the noseband about 2.5cm (1in) below the cheekbones. Never use halters on the delicate lower part of the horse's nose, and if there is any sign of rubbing at all, use a sheepskin guard to protect the horse's skin.

There are some halters on the market that even if they don't close down on the horse when the handler applies pressure, can still be very severe because they cut into the horse like cheese wire. As a general rule, the thinner and harder the material, the more severe the halter. If you have any reservations about what you are using on your horse, then put the halter around the back of your neck and ask someone to pull with a steady even pressure. If it hurts or cuts into you in any way, that is what it will feel like on your horse, so consider carefully whether you still want to use it.

Do also be careful that whatever you buy is of good quality and fits well, and isn't likely to slip around your horse's face or over an eye. If you take a look at some makes of halter, you can see that you can easily make one up yourself and probably do a better job.

Do plenty of pressure-release work on another human being before you start on a horse. You will find that humans are far less patient and

The horse needs to be able to separate your 'yes' from your 'no'.

*Case study*

## ALL DRUGGED UP

*One of the first remedial horses I ever helped Monty Roberts with was a little racehorse who had won his first race but the owner thought he hadn't jumped out of the stalls quickly enough so they brought him home and gave him electric shocks in the starting stalls to 'sharpen him up a bit'. Of course the next time they tried to put him in the starting stalls, it was hardly surprising that the little horse didn't want to go in. After more electric shocks and whipping the owner tried giving the horse some sedatives which didn't appear to do anything. So, I quote, 'We gave him enough to knock out an elephant', and they managed to push him in the starting stalls. This illustrates perfectly what fear, plus lack of inhibition can do, because the little fellow managed to smash those metal starting stalls completely to pieces, and break out before he eventually collapsed on the floor. This is when the owner decided he could do with some advice – if only people would ask sooner.*

understanding than horses. Ask them for their marks out of ten for your timing, feel and consistency – and don't be offended when they tell you the truth.

## THESE ARE NOT TRAINING AIDS

We need to be realistic about certain controversial 'tools' that are regularly used in the horse world. If there was some emergency that meant getting the horse to stand absolutely still right that second, I would use whatever methods were necessary to protect that horse. In this case it is very likely that you are working with the services of a vet who carries the necessary equipment and who will advise on its use.

However, do remember that not all vets have been taught how to use this equipment nor, more importantly, have they been made aware of better alternatives. These methods are not training aids, and if used thoughtlessly they can cause as many problems than they solve, as well as being potentially cruel and even very dangerous.

### TWITCHES

A 'twitch' squeezes hold of the horse's upper lip to make him stand quietly. The old fashioned type is a wooden 'pole' (a little thicker than a rolling pin) about 50cm (20in) long with a 13cm (5in) loop of orange string going through a hole in the end. You put the loop over your hand, hold the horse's nose, then pull the loop over on to the horse's nose and twist until it is holding the nose firmly. In an emergency you can make up a version using a hoof pick and some orange string.

Reading that description you may think it is just a brutal tool to force the horse to stand. However, there have been some interesting studies as related in Susan McBane's book *How to Cure Behaviour Problems in Horses*: 'The heart-rate of a twitched horse actually drops and the eyes take on a slightly glazed, far-away look. Neither of these are signs we would expect in a pain-ridden, panic-stricken animal; they are signs of relaxation. The twitched horse is, in fact, sedated by its own endorphins. The horse in agony has a high heart-rate, 60 beats per minute or more depending on the severity of the pain, and the same applies in situations of panic and fear. The Dutch team, led by Professor Lagerweij, believes that the upper lip/nose area is, in fact, an acupuncture or acupressure point which the inventors of the twitch accidentally discovered.'

It's quite correct that twitched horses do take on that same glazed look that seems to indicate release of endorphins.

However, while this might prove that the twitch isn't as bad as we might at first suppose, I have never known a horse that has had a twitch on look forward to having it on again. Generally speaking, once you have used it on a horse two or three times in his life, you are going to start to have difficulty getting it on again. As I stated before, the twitch may be acceptable in an emergency – say, for the vet, who will carry one in his or her car – but it is not acceptable for routine work such as clipping, farrier or worming. If you have general problems, to be fair on your horse, you need to work out the root causes and overcome these.

If you do ever have to use a twitch, make sure the edges of the horse's lips are turned under so they are not uncomfortable. Attach it firmly so that the horse can't slip out easily, and don't let go of the wooden part and have a horse throwing his head around with it swinging off the end of his nose – a sure way to get broken teeth and noses. Keep the twitch moving a little bit (just 'twitching') to encourage the flow of endorphins. Get the job done as quickly as possible and when you take the twitch off, give the horse's nose a rub to restore normal feeling. Don't ever, ever use a twitch round the horse's ear or any other sensitive part of his anatomy. This is a horrible practice. These areas don't release endorphins and you will cause permanent damage and behaviour problems.

## HUMANE HORSE HANDLER, COMMANCHE CALMER OR COMMANCHE TWITCH

This is a line that comes over the horse's poll, under the top lip and over the top teeth. It can be gradually tightened for greater control. This may be kinder than a twitch because you can use very light contact and only use stronger contact where necessary. I have heard of it being used successfully to manage emergency situations.

## CHIFNEY

This is a very severe bit often used on 'troublesome' racehorses and stallions. It is very effective because as soon as the horse realizes it can hurt, he walks very carefully alongside the handler. There is no pain involved unless, of course, it is pulled and misused. I never thought I would approve of the use of a chifney until I had to deal with a racehorse with a tendon injury and enforced box rest for three months. When he first came out of the box there was no way I could risk this horse even jumping around a little or he could go back to the beginning again. His early in-hand exercise was done on a chifney and wearing a side reins and a roller until he was passed fit by the vet to move more freely. Thankfully, long, enforced box rests are getting rarer and some of the 'enclosed-style' horse walkers that don't allow too much additional movement can be really helpful in circumstances like these.

## SEDATIVES

If you are under the impression that giving a sedative like ACP will solve all your problems because the horse will just go all sleepy and allow you to do anything you like – think again. The effects of ACP are particularly unpredictable and tend to ebb and flow. I have seen the kindest, calmest old horse ever known be doped because he didn't like being clipped, suddenly turn into a 'wild child', kicking everybody out of his stable. Just think about it, i.e. mixing fear or anger and adrenaline with a drug that loosens inhibitions, can produce some explosive results on occasions. There are times when sedatives can be helpful to manage certain situations, but don't be fooled that they can ever make a training aid. Doing something when you are 'drugged' doesn't constitute a learning experience.

## STALLION CHAINS

These are used by some people to exert extra control, and while possibly acceptable in the right hands, they can cause soreness and bruising to the skin if used roughly, which is to be avoided at all costs.

## HOLDING THE SKIN

This is when a fold of skin is simply lifted up in front of the shoulder, pinched and held firmly. Like the lip/nose area, this may be another acupressure point, and it often calms a horse, encouraging him to stand still for a while. However, it's obviously not comfortable for the horse, and you don't want him to become suspicious of you stroking him in that area. So only consider holding the skin for an emergency situation, and don't mistake it for a training aid.

### DON'T DO THIS AT HOME

I know of a top-class racehorse in a neighbouring yard who was one of the favourites for the Stewards Cup at Goodwood. The night before the race two stable lads thought they would smarten up the horse's mane and to make him stand still put a twitch on the horse's tongue. It's really too horrible to think about, but needless to say within a short time his tongue had blown up to twice its normal size and the poor horse wasn't able to run the next day or, indeed, for some time.

## HORSE SENSE

The trouble with 'horse sense' is that the horses seem to have it all. As I mentioned how our senses are getting less and less refined because we are learning to 'switch off' from our environment to a large extent, so we seem to be becoming more specialist in many areas and neglecting our common sense or 'horse sense' in other areas. We are getting to expect certain rules and regulations to protect us and it can come as a bit of a shock when everything doesn't go by these rules. I think one of the biggest dangers is putting total faith in 'experts', never questioning what they are saying. I believe we need to ask questions all the time, and also listen to ourselves more. If you have any doubts about what someone is telling you, research the information yourself, get a second opinion, tell them you don't understand and get them to explain it so you do understand. This can save you a lot of grief in the long run. Equally, if you are ever speaking as the 'expert', try to be as clear as possible.

## THIRD TIME LUCKY

A horse will usually understand within three tries – if this doesn't happen, you may have to face the possibility that you have not been showing him what you require in the most effective way. Indeed, you may even need to rethink your methods. This is actually the same with teaching human students. Thankfully, the old-style riding-school teachers who just shouted the same thing louder if the rider didn't understand, are being replaced by teachers with a more understanding and intelligent approach, who appreciate that if something isn't working you need

## ALL TRUE STORIES – MISUNDERSTANDINGS I HAVE KNOWN

• A vet says, 'Put a poultice on that horse's leg and I'll come and see him in a couple of weeks.' The owner thought the same poultice was to be left on for two weeks and by the time the vet returned, the horse had developed gangrene.

• A girl was advised to mouth a horse in side reins – she did this leaving the horse in side reins for 24 hours.

• A girl went to work in a racing yard in Newmarket. On her first day she was told to go to the bottom of the gallops and 'jump off' (meaning, let the horse go into a canter) and 'let him go' (meaning, let him go into a gallop). Unfortunately, not being conversant with racing lingo, the rider went to the bottom of the gallops as directed and took 'jump off' to mean 'get off' and 'let him go' to mean, well, 'let him go'. Happily they did manage to catch the horse safely.

to consider changing it. Unfortunately, the 'more of the same' approach has been a part of human and animal nature for millions of years, even bringing about the extinction of entire species. It's incredible how there is a tendency in us all to feel that if something worked once, then no matter how much the situation has changed, the same thing must surely work again.

A fairly intelligent approach is to keep doing something only if it continues to work. If it doesn't, try something else or remember: 'If at first you don't succeed, find someone who knows what they're doing'. Think about the goals you've been trying to accomplish and analyse your approach. Too often we bang our heads against a brick wall trying to make something happen even when we've received a clear message that what we're doing isn't working. This takes an enormous amount of precious time and energy.

It is essential that you allow a horse to learn by presenting a selection of options. You just make sure the option you want him to choose is the one that he is most likely to take. Horses are not naturally aggressive animals, and – as I've said before – if they are presented with several different options, presented correctly, they will nearly always take the path of least resistance.

## THE STAGES OF LEARNING

It has been suggested in learning theory that you pass through four very distinct stages. Just think about learning to drive a car. There is:

1 Unconscious incompetence.

2 Conscious incompetence.

3 Conscious competence.

4 Unconscious competence.

I hope this book will help you avoid to some extent the trap of stage 1 (unconscious incompetence) so that you are at least thinking carefully about what you are doing. However, generally stages 2 and 3 are necessary before getting to the blissful state of stage 4. What's important in learning, and indeed life, is not whether you can reach a point more quickly than everybody else, but whether you have the staying power to continue to study and improve and be the best that you can be. One of the best ways of learning that can sometimes happen without you even knowing it, is by being with people who are at the point where you want to be. Perhaps it's by some process of osmosis that you find yourself getting more like them. Do be careful, though: this process is just as effective for establishing negative traits.

## ATTITUDE IS EVERYTHING

If you take a careful look around the average livery yard or show, you will often see a lot of angry, unhappy people. Of course, there are angry, aggressive people in all walks of life. However, we name our courses 'Intelligent Horsemanship' and we feel that losing your temper is an uncontrolled, undisciplined act that can play no part in our work, and can certainly completely destroy the trust of a formerly good relationship. There have been times when I've mentioned to people that it is unacceptable to lose your temper with animals. They have more or less said that this philosophy is all right for superhumans and saints, but 'sometimes you just can't help yourself'. While I agree that it may well be natural for some people to lose their temper, particularly if they've experienced violence and temper tantrums while growing up themselves, it is possible to break the pattern if you commit yourself to the decision that this is what you are going to do.

A great deal of anger comes from frustration, and frustration

### PLEASE THINK

Anyone who's ever taken a walk down a road in the rain will know that in general people don't always think. Try it one day and you will find that nine out of ten car drivers will drive through the puddles right next to you and leave you drenched. Assuming they are not people who know you and have some reason for doing this, we can also assume that most people are not deliberately malicious either. It's just when there are no consequences for the action – i.e. the wet, soggy person can't do much about the situation – it seems most people don't give matters a great deal of thought. Make sure you don't treat your horse so thoughtlessly.

comes from thinking that you can't handle the problem presented. But supposing you were confident that you can solve whatever challenge you came across? Then you wouldn't get frustrated and you wouldn't get angry – simple! You could solve any problem that you had. Look at it this way – a quiet, intelligent person thinking through and looking at a problem from all angles (this is you, by the way) is far more likely to come up with a solution than some angry, screaming idiot (not you, but anyone you know?).

Next time a challenge arises, don't get angry, or use the easy option to attack the horse in some way. Pause and say to yourself, 'I know I can work this out.' If you can stand apart from the situation for a while, all the better: maybe even jot down some notes or discuss possible solutions with a perceptive friend.

Be clear in your mind what it is you want to achieve. Then think, 'How can I make it easy and comfortable for him to do what I want him to do?' 'What am I doing that this horse doesn't understand?' Think what you can achieve on the right path in the short term.

From observing people, it seems that some feel they should be angry when there's a problem. Again, this is a dilemma that needs analysing. Certainly, if you are a competition rider you should care whether you give a bad or below-par performance, but anger will immobilize you, preventing you from finding better answers. So don't choose it!

Is anger ever useful? Possibly if you get annoyed with yourself and don't try to put the blame on others, it can serve a purpose. I have also sometimes found it helpful to 'act' somewhat aggressively in circumstances where I need additional strength, for instance if I am schooling a particularly tough horse on the ground. Not being particularly strong or heavy, I sometimes need to put a fair amount of effort into my 'assertive' movements to be effective. To be angry, though, would be counter-productive.

> Remember: we have horses for fun – it's an expensive way to be miserable.

Be wary too of 'displacement' (see also Behaviourism for Beginners, page 215). This refers to a shift of emotion away from the person or object causing the anger towards what one feels is a more neutral or less dangerous object. For example, you're upset by the person you work for, so you come home and take it out on a member of your family or your horse.

Not infrequently, the smallest incident may serve as the trigger that releases all the pent-up emotion in a torrent of displaced anger and abuse. Anyone in a 'weaker' position – for example, animals, children, or people who are financially tied to the aggressor in some way, are ideal candidates because they can't fight back. I bet there aren't many people who will pick on a prize boxer, saying, 'I just lost my temper – I couldn't help myself', because they'd be well aware of the possibility of unpleasant reprisals. Much more sensible, it seems, to 'lose it' with your

## TWELVE TIPS FOR STAYING CALM

**1** Analyse why you get angry. Could it be frustration, displacement, fear, embarrassment, incompatibility or stress?

**2** Face up to your anger.

**3** Deal with the real issue.

**4** Learn to breathe correctly.

**5** Make a contract with yourself to eliminate violence as an option.

**6** Think how you are going to act if there is a chance your temper could be tested. Visualize yourself acting with complete integrity.

**7** Keeping your cool doesn't mean being weak: just the opposite. You can be far more effective if you keep your wits about you.

**8** Accept that people will actually admire you far more if you keep your cool. Play the admiring comments of people in your head.

**9** Don't deal with your horse when you're so tired, stressed, hungry or unhappy that you know you can't do him justice.

**10** If you feel yourself getting worked up, take time out until you feel calm enough to deal with things more intelligently.

**11** Don't carry a whip if you think there's a chance you are going to use it in temper rather that just as an additional signalling system. The giddy-up rope works better and you need to use it in a pretty controlled fashion for best effect – a good discipline for you.

**12** Be kind to your horse and yourself. Appreciate both of your good points frequently.

horse or child – but it's time those people faced up to the fact that they're bullies as well as cowards.

In a similar way, some people who are frightened of horses, or get embarrassed easily, express anger at the horse instead of admitting the real reason to themselves or anyone else. Consequently, it is the horses that suffer until these people face up to their real feelings and take more appropriate steps.

If you find you are generally very good-natured but get irritated with one particular horse on a consistent basis, you may have to face up to the fact that you are not compatible. It happens. Do both of you a favour and find a horse more suited to your temperament and abilities.

### STRESS RELIEF

Another cause of anger is stress spilling over from other areas of your life. Are you finding yourself getting angry about many things just lately? A health check should be your first stop; your doctor can talk to you about whether you are eating correctly and sleeping enough. If you are in a stressful job, you must learn how to put all that behind you before spending time with your horse. There are so many good alternative remedies for horses: homeopathy, aromatherapy, massage, acupuncture. Think about it, maybe it isn't so much your horse that needs these treatments as much as you do.

Another important stress reliever is to work on your breathing. Correct breathing is so important on a number of different levels. If your breathing is calm, even and steady, then, to a degree, your mind experiences these same qualities. If the lower abdominal muscles are relaxed during inhalation, there is more room for the diaphragm to move down,

*Case study*

# WHO NEEDS THE REMEDY?

*A lady called Nora phoned me in a distressed state. Her 17hh TB horse wouldn't go in his stable. He'd been away for an operation and on his return he was at a new yard where the door of the stable was narrow and the overhang low. I gave her some advice and promised to attend the following day. After all my advice on the phone, by the time I arrived Nora already had him going in and out quite calmly. I stayed a while and gave some further advice. Nora was a big worrier so as we were chatting I suggested she might try some 'de-stress' ideas such as lavender oil and other remedies.*

*A few days later I got another call from Nora, saying, 'Help – he won't go in the trailer to go for his therapy swim.' He had always loaded and travelled well before. Nora admitted she'd got stressed because they were running late and that had transferred to the horse and now he wouldn't load. So, once again, I travelled to the yard. I worked with the horse and Nora. She was confidently loading him by the end of the session.*

*The next day I received a phone message from Nora's husband, Paul. 'He went straight in!' he cried. 'Thank you so much for all your help. Also Nora is so much calmer with everything now. The only real complaint is – the whole house stinks of lavender!'*

**INTELLIGENT HORSEMANSHIP RECOMMENDED ASSOCIATE HANNAH ROSE**

and more air is taken into the lungs. Make your breathing long, slow, calm and deep. When you inhale, expand not only your chest but your upper and lower abdomen as well. You can breathe more fully and are therefore more energized. There is a strong connection between your breathing, your mind and emotions. For example, when a person gets angry they tend to hold their breath, and when someone gets anxious or panics, their breath tends to get shorter and shallower.

Breathing is the only way you can fully oxygenate your body and stimulate the electrical process of each cell – including your brain cells. Lower abdominal breathing also helps keep the centre of gravity low and is associated with calmness and relaxation. One of the best ways to start relaxation training is meditation sitting or lying down. Yoga and martial arts training also include excellent relaxation techniques.

## USING FOOD IN YOUR TRAINING

Food is quite a controversial subject in horse training. While some people say it should never be used, there are others who feel it is the only worthwhile reinforcement. I think you need to look at the pros and cons, then try and make a balanced judgement and decide the best way forward with the particular horse and case in question. Remember, horses, like people, are all born different as well as having different histories. A method that is perfect for one may not be right for another.

## THE DISADVANTAGES OF USING FOOD AS A TRAINING AID

- It can encourage biting and nibbling.
- Some horses (particularly little ponies) can become overexcited if there is food around and totally lose focus on the handler.
- It can even be dangerous dealing with a horse that has ever been starved, or if, for instance, you take a bucket of feed to catch a horse in a field full of horses.
- It can encourage wood biting.
- Horses don't see food as a reward in the same way that dogs and seals do. Dog and seals, being predators, have it in their nature to 'capture' food, to link the 'kill' with the 'reward'. Horses are used to having food around and don't regard it as a reward in quite the same way.

## CLICKER TRAINING

This is a system of pairing a food reward with a clicker noise, made from a tiny hand-held box you can buy. It was originally devised for dolphins and seals and has lately been developed for horses.

To use the clicker, you get a horse to touch a specific 'target' (it doesn't matter if it only happens accidentally at first) and you give a food reward and 'click' at the same time. In time the horse gets to connect the click with the reward and soon learns even when the food isn't present that if he hears the click it means he's given the right response.

As I discussed earlier, horses don't seem to understand food rewards in the same way as dogs do, and although this should be a humane method, it's not as easy as it might at first seem. Now that dog owners have caught on to the idea of clicker training, professional dog trainers are being brought dogs that have been confused and essentially taught the opposite of what was intended by the owner's misuse of clickers. This is not the fault of the method but the fault of the owner's timing and consistency. This problem arises in any horse training too, of course, and what we need to do is never blame the horse but keep looking at ourselves and thinking, 'How can I improve to enable this horse to understand and learn better?'

## THE ADVANTAGES OF USING FOOD AS A TRAINING AID

- Food is a primary reinforcer, i.e. it's not something a horse has to learn to appreciate, such as praise or even stroking from humans. It's a totally natural incentive for them and if a horse is hungry food can be useful to coax him somewhere. For instance, if a horse is severely frightened of the trailer because of a previous bad experience, you can leave the trailer in his field with hay just inside.
- Your horse seeing you bringing in and supplying his food and water may make him appreciate you more.
- Food is undoubtedly a pleasant association for the horse. If he knows a feed is always waiting there, it gives him a good reason to come into his stable when asked or to want to go into the horsebox.
- Food gives the horse another good reason to look forward to seeing you.

• Food can be a useful distraction. If emergency measures are needed, it is far better to distract a horse with food during a quick injection from the vet, for instance than start struggling with twitches or other restraining aids.
• If a horse is chewing, it's relaxing for him.
• Getting a horse to bend his head around to follow a carrot is a good physiotherapy exercise.
• There are some horse trainers now finding success using food with 'clicker training' (see box opposite).
• Food is very effective for getting horses to prick their ears for photographs and showing classes.
• It's an extra 'tool' you have available.

## WHAT ABOUT THE OCCASIONAL TREAT?

I enjoy attending other trainers' clinics, and the subject of why you should never give your horse food as a treat was brought up at one I was attending. I have to admit, it didn't leave me altogether convinced. The young trainer said he would never give his horses food rewards because, 'It's like with my girlfriend. If I were to give her chocolates and flowers every time I saw her, then I wouldn't know if she was pleased to see them rather than me.' He continued: 'In the same way, I want to know the horse is only interested in what I want him to do – not what I might give him.' A couple of other girls in the audience and I agreed that he may have had a point, but we were left with this vague feeling that being his girlfriend (or horse) may not be a great deal of fun.

Concerns about feeding by hand are justified because it can encourage biting, nibbling and even 'mugging'. The rule here is only to ever offer the food when the horse is standing respectfully away from you. Never give food as a 'reward' for horses that go into your pockets, as this can escalate into the horse pushing you around for food. Don't even consider feeding by hand if a horse is pushy or disrespectful in any way.

It's up to you to judge if it is doing your horse's behaviour any harm or not. If I were going to feed a treat at all, I'd also always try and make it something healthy, like an apple, rather than mints or sugar lumps. It's been found that very sweet treats can encourage biting wood as horses try and 'find the taste' again. You sometimes see dogs continue to lick their dish long after their food has been finished and they may go on to lick the floor afterwards. The closest human analogy I can think of is when you finish your ice lolly and continue to suck the stick.

## THE USE OF YOUR VOICE IN TRAINING

Talking to your horse as you spend time with him is one of the great pleasures of having a horse. Having an understanding listener who never interrupts or contradicts is undoubtedly of immeasurable benefit to our mental health and stress levels. I don't suggest for one moment that you permanently stop chatting to your horse as part of your daily routine, because although a horse may not actually understand what you are saying, it still may be of benefit as it may help you be clearer and more congruent in your actions. It can also help you control your fears more easily. Singing is a great help for nervous riders. If your tone of voice is calm and relaxed it may go some way to calming and relaxing both yourself and the horse. However, if you are having some training difficulties I would suggest it's a good idea to examine whether your talking is part of the solution or part of the problem.

Where I find the use of the rider's voice is really a hindrance is when people believe the horse does and should understand every word they are saying. The problem here is that it may be stopping the person doing something more effective. While the person is keeping themselves occupied by going, 'Silly boy, no, naughty, no, stop that at once now', they are not thinking about doing something that will make a difference.

Another point is that the words you use should be important for you, as well as for the horse. Think about the effect on your feelings if you are to tell your horse that he is 'stupid', 'silly', 'an idiot'. Does it relax you and put you in a good frame of mind for working with that horse? It

**SMELLS TASTY**

FOOD IS VERY EFFECTIVE FOR GETTING HORSES TO PRICK THEIR EARS FOR PHOTOGRAPHS.

*Case study*

# JUST LISTEN TO ME!

*Recently I was asked to do a Join Up with a lovely racehorse called Jack who was giving his trainer some problems. Jack had been lunging a great deal and had only been allowed to slow down on voice commands. A horse like this will often think it's wrong to even look at the handler, so I used my voice just to slow him down and get him to look at me, and as he looked at me I gave my submissive/invitational body language and we carried on the process. It would have been unfair on the horse if I had been dogmatic: 'That's not the way I do Join Up; you must do it my way'. By making some allowances it permitted us to begin to develop an understanding on that first day. The next day his new attitude was just stunning. This bond and understanding came right through to his ridden work and, after some advice to his lad, it meant he actually agreed to go up to the gallops for the first time in months.*

often does the opposite. That's why I sometimes suggest people stop talking to their horse for a week or so while they are working on any problems to enable them to get clear in their mind what they are actually trying to achieve and how vocal communication may help.

Horses' hearing is superior to ours, and thought to be only a little less acute than dogs. With 16 muscles in each ear and a mobility of 180 degrees with each ear working separately, they have a wonderful ability to pinpoint exactly where a noise is coming from. We can see where their attention is focused by looking at their ears. The external ears are built to pick up the slightest noise and precisely locate its source. By comparing the vibrations being funnelled into each ear, the location of even very distant signals can be pinpointed with remarkable accuracy. Horses can detect a far greater range of sounds at both the higher and lower ends of the frequency scale. Do try to be sympathetic to this when speaking in a high-pitched

## THE CLEVER HANS STORY

Hans was a horse living in Berlin in the early 20th century. He became famous for his ability to count and tell the time. He would count out the solutions to maths problems by pawing the ground with a front foot. His trainer, an elderly schoolmaster by the name of Wilhelm von Osten, firmly believed in clever Hans's genius.

It was only after a commission was sent by the Prussian Academy of Sciences that the truth was revealed. Hans wasn't able to get the right answer if no one in the area knew it. It was discovered that Hans closely observed the people watching him. They would tense up as he came to the right number and Hans realized this was his 'cue' to stop. In one version of the story I read, it said that von Osten was so embarrassed by Hans's 'deception' that he immediately got rid of him. What a horrible thought. Personally, I think the horse was even more clever than they thought in the first place – most people can count, after all, but how many people do you know who can read body language so accurately?

voice or if you're practising any whistling repertoires. One of the most irritating habits people can have is making the 'clucking' noise constantly. It is generally a noise used to raise the horse's pulse rate and has its uses for putting a little pressure on a horse, and yet you see people use it even when they are asking a horse to stand still. It's as if they are trying to communicate with a chicken.

Whether their superior hearing means horses can analyse the syllables from human speech as quickly as we can (or whether indeed they really want to pay attention to all our chat) seems unlikely. Every horse needs to get to know his or her name by being addressed by it regularly. It is disrespectful to have a horse around and not acknowledge 'who he is'. You can teach a horse to come to call. This is particularly useful if you fall off and I've known of people using it to advantage.

Voice commands undoubtedly can be effective, as shown particularly by the driving people, and they are a very useful additional communication aid.

In the same spirit, of letting the horse and your own intelligence guide you as to what to do (rather than thinking the horse 'should' do this or you 'should' do that), you need to be realistic about the effectiveness of word commands in certain circumstances. If a horse's adrenaline is up because of fear or excitement, be prepared to have a back-up system as some horses seem to acquire temporary deafness under stress.

Vocal communication is not the horse's first language. For practical purposes, it's generally the sociable, forest-dwelling animals that have the most elaborate vocal signals. Evolving from the open plains, by contrast, horses have developed a sophisticated range of visual signals to

*Case study*

## SCREAMING AND SCREECHING

*I visited a very nice lady and her pony recently. The problem they had was leading and a little bit of nipping – nothing too serious, but she just wanted him to pay her some more (positive) attention and gain more control. As I started to do some leading work with him and he proved a very bright student, the lady said, 'I can't believe how quickly he's improved and how well he's behaving now and I also find it interesting that you don't use voice commands.' I explained that until I got him to respond to what I was asking in his own language, as it were, that there wouldn't be much point in me using voice commands because they wouldn't mean anything to him. She said, 'Do you know, that makes so much sense.' She continued: 'Sometimes I go home exhausted because he just ignores what I've been telling him and by the end of the day I realize I've been screaming and shouting at him for hours!'*

meet most of their needs. Horses primarily read your body language when you are on the ground and your body movements when you are riding them. Frequently people underestimate just how clever horses are at picking out the tiniest movements and may believe the horse is responding to their words when, in fact, they are picking up visual or kinetic clues. Remember, horses are far better at 'reading' us than we are at reading them.

## KEY POINTS FOR VOICE TRAINING

• When training use the word at the time the horse is doing what you ask so he connects the word with the action. For instance, if you want to teach your horse the verbal command 'whoa', one method is to walk your horse head on towards a fence, tighten your abdominal muscles as you come towards the fence, and still your seat bones and say 'Whoa' just at the moment the horse naturally stops.

• You mustn't apply wishful thinking in the initial training stage, saying 'whoa' just because you'd like him to stop. You say it *as* he stops so that he can connect what he's doing with the voice command. When he fully understands, that's when you can start using the verbal command as a request.

• Use the same word clearly each time. Don't say 'Whoa' one day, 'Stop' the next and 'Steady' the day after. Decide what you want each word to mean. It's also practical to work with one word (or sound) for 'slower' and one for 'faster', to work right through the gaits.

• Always keep things simple and clear.

• With all training methods, timing, consistency and consideration are the key. As with other methods, human failings are the biggest reason for voice training being ineffective.

• If you are going to use 'Good Boy' as a reward (conditioned stimulus) pair it up with pleasant things for your horse, like when you give him his feed, he's drinking or when you get off him, and then only use it when you really mean he's been good. Though praise and reassurance are often very similar in horse training, try to use the expression just for praise.

• Sometimes just the tone of your voice will be enough to reassure your horse. It doesn't matter much what you say – for example, 'You funny old thing!' – but if you are saying it lovingly and reassuringly your horse will feel better. However, if you are nervous and talk in a very high-pitched, squeaky voice to your horse, you will transmit your feelings even more clearly to your horse and serve to make him more anxious. It is better to keep quiet until you've got your own nerves under control.

• If you are nervous and find talking to yourself helps calm your nerves, here are ideas that people have found useful: one is to talk to your horse as if he is the one who is nervous and to tell him exactly what you plan

> **WARNING**
>
> The most common names for the 'special needs' horses that come to us are Deadly, Rocket, Striker, Kevin and Tyson. Be warned!

to do and reassure him about it all. You are really reassuring yourself, of course, but by taking this 'adult role' and concentrating on the horse, you will find that it takes the emphasis off what you are worrying about. Singing, I have heard, works wonderfully for nervous riders, concentrating their breathing as well as their minds. Also try positive affirmations – such as, 'I am a confident rider' – as they can help enormously.

## BEING ON OPPOSITE SIDES

It's very damaging to constantly have the attitude that you and your horse are somehow on opposites sides. It is difficult if you believe that you and your horse are engaged in some sort of battle and there is going to be a winner and a loser. The horse is just a horse: he has no secret agenda to 'beat' you or 'make a fool of you'; that's simply your own neurosis. He just looks at that trailer, river, track and can think of no good reason to go down there. It's up to you to persuade him differently, not through punishment but by finding a way to get him to want to do it.

## PERSUASIVE TACTICS

We need to ask ourselves, 'How can I get this horse to want to do this?' A tried and tested way is by giving the horse two options, making one (what you want him to do) very easy and the other slightly uncomfortable in the form of work for him. For instance, with a sluggish horse you may ask him to go just in small circles if he wants to hang round close to home, but make it very easy and pleasant for him once he starts to go out on the ride.

Training halters, used correctly, can be excellent for loading a reluctant horse into a trailer by clearly separating your 'Yes' from your 'No' and making what you want the horse to do an easy choice. However, it's an injustice to the horse if we get so set on any 'system' that we close our minds to possibly better alternatives for use at different times. When working with a horse you need to think, 'Am I making this situation better or worse?' If you feel you are getting further away from your goals, think of other methods of getting the horse to understand the best way to go. It's human nature to do 'more of the same'; if something doesn't work just apply more pressure – hit harder, push harder, pull

> ## THE BASIC WORDS YOUR HORSE NEEDS TO UNDERSTAND
> • His name.
> • 'Good Boy', for when he's got it right. Stroke and pet him at the same time initially.
> • 'Up' for picking any leg up.
> • 'Over' for moving over in the stable, horsebox or at any other time.
> • 'Back'.
> • 'Stand'.
> • 'Whoa'.
> You have a choice of teaching individual words for walk, trot, canter or you can just use one word for slower (maybe 'whoa') and one word for faster (may be a click or a kiss noise).

BATTING ON THE SAME SIDE THERE ARE TIMES WHEN WE CAN TRUST A HORSE, TIMES WHEN WE CAN'T AND TIMES WHEN WE HAVE TO.

## 'NERVES OR JUST NAUGHTY – HOW CAN YOU TELL?'

A common question I am asked, as if it is going to melt away all further difficulties with horses, is, 'How can you tell if your horse is genuinely frightened of something or is just "taking the mickey"/having you on/ being naughty?' The reason I find it hard to give a short answer to the 'frightened or naughty?' question is because, for many people, once they have established that the horse is not frightened and therefore being 'naughty' – it immediately means punishment is justified. So, for instance, if someone invited you round to their house for drinks, and you said, 'No, thanks', and they established that it wasn't because you were frightened, does it mean they would be perfectly justified in labelling you awkward, in screaming and shouting abuse at you, and perhaps even hitting you as well? Can you see there may be a better way for them to achieve the results they want?

I can give you an easy rule of thumb for telling if a horse is frightened or not – if he is, you will feel his heart beating much faster. You don't need to take a pulse reading, although it is a useful skill to have with horses. With sufficient experience you can see a horse's breathing and pulse rate go up even when you are standing some distance away. When you are riding, you can feel his heart rate even through the saddle. Another general guideline is that the more pressure you put on the horse – hitting, pulling and pushing – the more frightened he will become, and the more dramatically he will be likely to resist.

If a horse is frightened, we have to help him overcome that fear, for instance, with a horse that is frightened of loading in a trailer, trying to analyse exactly what the fear is and setting up small goals for him, such as leading him over a wooden bridge, taking him under a tarpaulin, leaving the trailer in the field and putting his feeds on the ramp (see pages 182–95). If the horse is not frightened but still doesn't want to do as we ask, we've got to find a way to get him to want to do as we ask.

Now you may well say that as you feed, muck out, groom this horse in all types of weather, as well as paying enormous bills on his behalf, he ought to do what you say. Unfortunately, money not only can't buy you love, but all your hard work (this will be familiar to parents as well) doesn't necessarily mean your horse is going to show constant gratitude by thinking up ways to show his appreciation.

harder. But we can do a much better job for ourselves, and the horse, if we aim at a more intelligent approach.

My horse Pie (more formally known as American Pie) put me in mind of this when I first started working with him for some of the photographs that appear in this book. It has been literally years since I've had my own horse at home – I've been concentrating on working with and riding other people's instead. I used to imagine that if I ever did get my own horse again he would be about 16.2hh, a handsome dark bay, perhaps. Yes, like many women, I was looking for tall, dark and handsome, and what happens but this funny little (15hh) Irish fellow (a 'paint', Monty calls him) turns up that's been bucking people off and very spooky. It was love ...

So Pie and I are on a ride and I decide we should go down a hill through some water and up the other side. Pie obviously thinks this is a bad idea. I stand and let him look for a while and put some pressure on with my legs. Resistance starts and I stop before he goes backwards 'into' the pressure, which is the natural instinct of horses. I didn't have a giddy-up rope to apply a gentle flicking motion, which can be very useful to encourage forward motion on a horse, so I picked a twig with some leaves on (actually often ideal to just 'tickle' a horse on) and tickled him with that behind my leg. This immediately upset him. I felt his heart rate go up and he started to hunch himself up to buck. 'It's OK,' I thought. 'No point in upsetting him. I know what works in this case. I'll just lead him.' I only ride him in a headcollar anyway, so it was easy enough to work using pressure and release just to ease him from side to side to bring him forward. Except he wasn't coming forward. I then, on a whim, picked some garlic leaves that were beside me, held them in front of Pie's nose and, before a second was up, Pie was down the hill in the water, and ecstatically sniffing the garlic leaves!

In cases like this, it's so nice to work on your own, with nobody shouting advice, no matter how well-meaning. I know there are people that would insist if they saw you in the situation I was in that you must stay on him:
• 'Show him who's boss.'
• 'Never use bribery or he'll know he's won.'
All the time such comments do nothing better than perpetuate the idea that the horse is an opponent you are trying to beat. Maybe there are cases when they would have a point. The reason I know I did absolutely the right thing on that occasion, is that the next day when we came to the hill that went down into the river, Pie hesitated for less that half a second before going straight on down and in. See the photograph on page 30, which illustrates a contented horse and rider successfully negotiating said hurdle. Since then I've asked Pie to do increasingly daring things and each time he's reacted with more and more confidence in me. I haven't had to get off again (or use garlic leaves), which seems to indicate we're heading in the right direction.

*Who knows what other tests Pie and I might face in our time together. Certainly it's a big responsibility – and I know it's up to me to keep on earning his trust.*

# *foundation* EXERCISES

What do you notice in a badly-mannered horse? Often his handler's lack of control – they can't get the horse to move where they want
him to, or stop him from moving in too close. The horse has no respect
for the person's space, and no respect for their requests. These are the
first things to address in your training work. All the most respected
schools of horsemanship, from the Spanish riding school Cadre Noir,
Nuno Olivera, to North American trainers such as Tom Dorrance, Ray
Hunt and Monty Roberts, have known that the starting point for most
remedial horses is with the handler working him initially from the
ground.

Something I have found when meeting many 'remedial' horses night
after night on demonstration tours is that they can be very 'wooden'.
Sometimes, I'll work with a horse that's ridden but won't load into a
horsebox or, say, a horse that is intermittently nappy. To start with, I
may not be able to touch the horse in certain areas of his head or body
and won't be able to get him to take even half a step backwards without putting in a lot of effort. I often wonder how the owner has
managed to do any ridden work with the horse at all. Going out on a
horse that doesn't have the basic training of being able to bend, to yield
and understand how to move away from pressure, is like going out in a
car with no steering, no brakes and the electricity is shorting. Sometimes the horse's owners guiltily confess they are nervous of riding the
horse. I tell them they are entitled to be.

What are the biggest sensitivity destroyers? Heavy, hard hands,
heavy, hard legs and a heavy, hard voice – none of these gives your
horse the opportunity to respond to a light aid because there are no
light aids. At every moment you need to read your horse. If he's not
responding well, you need to judge if he is putting up defences and why.
This often comes from a horse being uncomfortable and being asked to
do too much or more than he understands, which results in confusion.

EASY DOES IT
TEACHING YOUR HORSE TO
LOWER HIS HEAD MAKES
EVERYDAY HANDLING MUCH
EASIER.

A horse will also become defensive if he is afraid of punishment; his mind will only be focusing on when the pain is likely to come. Punishment will make the problem worse. Be aware that the naturally sensitive horse perceives he's been punished far more readily than the more stoic type. It doesn't matter if you didn't mean to punish him or 'barely' touched him – if he believes he's been punished, then to him he has been. Remember, the more tense a horse is, the more he will brace himself against pressure – whether it's coming from the bit, your legs, whip or anywhere else. If you think this negative cycle may be happening with your horse, the best route is to take him right back to basics.

## CONTROLLING YOUR HORSE'S MOVEMENTS

Horses work best with clear and consistent boundaries, and unless they have no respect or confidence in their handler, are usually happy to follow instructions if they understand them. A horse should be happy with you touching him all over – with no ticklish or 'no go' areas at all. Once that is established, you need to be sure you have control of all your horse's movements on the ground – forwards, backwards, sideways, standing still and, most importantly, maintaining a respectful distance from you unless otherwise invited.

### CONTROLLING THE SITUATION

If you were riding a horse that started to take control you'd be wise to execute some half-halts, changes of direction, small circles or rein back to 'bring him back' to you. On the ground you have the option of loose work in the round pen, halter work or long lining. In this work it has to be you that is clearly in charge of changing the direction and soon you will feel the resistance replaced by a softening, more receptive attitude.

How horses show dominance in the herd – in fact, the only way horses can show dominance in the herd – is by controlling the 'lesser' horses' movements. Consequently, it follows that every time he pushes you around or moves you away, the less he respects you. Just the action of moving a horse around a little can change his whole attitude to human beings.

You must be able to manoeuvre your horse around easily. This will improve his spatial awareness, and once he starts to consider where you are, you can spend less time manoeuvring him off your feet. These exercises can be started with a weanling (but keep lessons short) or done with any older horse that may benefit. It is an excellent idea to work through these exercises with a young horse before starting him.

### PRESSURE AND RELEASE

The concept of pressure and release will be used throughout these exercises and very often throughout the book. The horse has to be able to distinguish your 'Yes' from your 'No'. The clearest way for you to show him is by applying a little pressure and, as soon as he yields, immedi-

*Case study*

## 'DOMINANT' HORSES

*On my demonstration tour of Europe in 1999 (ten venues in Holland, Belgium, Luxembourg and Germany) I was demonstrating how to deal with common horse and handler problems. At three different venues I was handed a horse for the demonstration by some worried-looking owner who labelled their animal as 'extremely dominant'. As it was led up to the arena, the horse would be walking or jogging at least a stride ahead of the handler, which made it uncomfortable for both of them. Uncomfortable for the handler, as he or she was being pushed around and trodden on, and uncomfortable for the horse, as the handler was getting in the way of his body and feet as he tried to look round and work out what was going on – not a good situation.*

*Certainly, these horses could be described as 'dominant' in that, as in the dictionary definition, they held a 'commanding position over another'. Whether this was some inborn characteristic or whether, indeed, it was in any way desirable to the horse, I feel was strongly debatable.*

*The 'dominant' horses I met on the European trip all showed very clear signs of anxiety. They needed someone to take over the responsibility to relieve their anxiety. The best way of getting a horse to listen to you, whether when riding or on the ground, is to start to direct and control his movements. This goes back to herd behaviour where the lead horses show their superiority by directing the other horses' movements, whether in or out of the herd.*

*In each case, the horse proved not dominant at all but insecure and anxious because of his owner's indecision. The poor horse was simply saying, 'I'm just a horse. I have to decide where we go, what we do AND I have to cope with this person getting under my feet.' As soon as the owners took some responsibility, the horses responded beautifully and visibly relaxed.*

ately releasing it, so that he understands he has done the right thing. A feeling for your horse and split-second timing are essential because that is the only way the horse can understand what it is he needs to do in order to release the pressure.

Intelligence in a horse is not always seen as an advantage by many horsepeople, and is clearly a disadvantage if the horse is more intelligent than his handler. Similarly, sensitivity is a double-edged sword, which, it must be clear, is a quality that needs to be developed in both of you or not at all.

Charles Darwin remarked that women may be more intuitive than men to make up for their lack of strength. Obviously this is a big generalization, but, in the same vein, it's noticeable that the more delicately made a horse is, the more sensitive he seems to be to any stimulus.

These exercises can help develop sensitivity in your horse. They will give him an interest and encourage him to listen to what you ask. On the other hand, if you feel your horse is 'over-sensitive' it's possible that these exercises can increase *your* sensitivity to help you be a better

The 3 'R's of horsemanships:
Request
Response
Release

# MONTY ROBERTS WATCHES KELLY MARKS

Recently I was taken to a riding school in Germany. There was to be a demonstration that evening conducted by a student of mine. I spent a captivating three hours watching Kelly Marks work with horses and people at the same time. Kelly handled three equine students in an effort to give them a better understanding of how to lead a comfortable and fun-filled life with humans. She simultaneously worked with her audience with the hope that they would see and appreciate the value of the concepts that she was utilizing.

One of Kelly's subjects was a very large chestnut mare who had a well-known aversion to loading on to trailers. Any horseperson could see at once that there was no respect for humans between those ears of hers. This was a German warm-blood with all of the attributes of her breed: heavy bones, big feet, 17hh and the power of Godzilla. And there was Kelly, less than nine stone and looking more like a doll fixed on the end of the leadline.

The mare was described by the owner as 'dominant', even aggressive. As Kelly worked, you could easily see that 'dominant' was spelled S-P-O-I-L-E-D. This mare had been trained to take advantage of people by giving her positive consequences for negative actions. Like so many children, she had become phobic in her need to control people. In my opinion, this mare was now very unhappy and didn't even know why. She was compelled to fight because of the environment she had come from.

Kelly needed a schooling halter to give her any chance of handling this mare. It was a challenge just to lead her, let alone load her. Within 10 minutes, though, Kelly was getting through to this huge terrorist. Giving praise and reward at the moment it was appropriate and schooling quickly when it was called for, Kelly made great progress. She was approaching the trailer in about 15 minutes. With the use of the halter combined with Join Up (see pages 86-107), Kelly was loading and unloading within the next three to five minutes.

I watched the mare lick and chew, lead willingly, and respect Kelly as they worked in a co-operative fashion. This mare was not 'dominant' or 'aggressive'. She was spoiled. Kelly reasoned with her in her own language and changed her attitude in a matter of minutes. There was no hitting or even raising a voice to this mare.

One woman was heard to say, 'I saw Monty Roberts last year but I did not believe that I could do what he teaches. After watching Kelly I am convinced that I too can do it.' It is my hope that more people will come to this conclusion. Unless horsepeople of all descriptions can successfully use my concepts, it will not be possible to reach my life's goal – to leave the world a better place than I found it, both for horses and people.

**MONTY ROBERTS**

handler for him. As you become more polished with these techniques, you will find how useful they are in everyday situations. For instance, they will enable you to place a horse's feet exactly as you wish in show classes and photographs, without having to go near the horse. You will use them when you're getting on your horse or waiting to go through a gate on a ride. The advanced backing-up technique is a useful prerequisite for 'Ground Tying' (see page 126). You can use these exercises as tools to improve communication with your horse as well as remembering that horses 'learn to learn' – reinforcement for his neural pathways.

## COMING-FORWARD EXERCISE
**Aim:** To come towards you off a long rope, coming right up to you from from 3m (10ft) away or further.

1 To start with, work from a 45-degree angle in front of your horse and gradually ask him to come forward. If he still resists, take a step to the side to make the angle more acute.

**COMING-FORWARD**

IT IS BEST TO ASK YOUR HORSE TO COME TOWARDS YOU OFF A LONG ROPE.

2 Once you are at a 90-degree angle, your horse can't help but move because you are able to unbalance him from his position. This is just as a way of showing him that you can control his movement and that pressure from the rope means movement. Remember to release the pressure as soon as he thinks about making any definite movement.

For this exercise make sure that you are not looking the horse in the eye and keep your body at a slight angle, i.e. not an aggressive stance (although make sure you are still in a position to put pressure on the rope). Remember, just because you are not looking the horse in the eye, it doesn't mean you're not seeing everything that's going on. You'll probably have your gaze directed vaguely at his chest area.

### BACKING-UP EXERCISE
**Aim:** To teach the horse to back up.

1 Hold the rope directly underneath the headcollar and stand in front of him although slightly to one side. You can alternate this to make use of both arms. As you take a step towards him, give a series of short pushes on the rope until he takes a step backwards. You can couple this with a 'kissing' noise.

2 Stop pushing, and give him a moment of relaxation and perhaps a head rub to reward him, as soon as he takes the smallest step back. Don't expect him to go completely straight in the early stages; that will come later.

Keep these lessons short and soon he will realize instantly what the pressure means even if it is only from a single finger. Quite soon he will learn that as you take a step towards him in an assertive manner and/or make the kiss noise, he should take a step away.

## WORKING WITH ROPES AND LINES

If ever you find yourself with a horse that is much stronger than you and pulling away, rather than risk permanently (that means for the rest of your life) damaging the ligaments in your arms and shoulders, I advise you to let the horse go.

Learn from the experience. Were you holding the rope too short so you couldn't get any leverage? Did you allow the horse to get too far directly in front of you so you couldn't get at the right angle to pull him round and stop him? Did you have the most suitable type of halter on him? Was he just madly over fresh? One of the benefits of working in a safe, enclosed area while you are figuring these things out, is that even if you do let the horse go, he won't even be aware of it if he can't go too far.

If you step away from him with eyes lowered and your arms together, he should step towards you. If you want him to stand in one place as you back off, give him eye contact and keep your arms open wide.

### If it's not happening
Make sure you are only asking for one step at a time, in the early stages. If you carry on pushing as he backs up, and only stop when he stops,

you'll be teaching him to resist. Continue to work on other methods to free your horse's actions for a few days and then, from time to time, try to back him again. It's not rare to find yourself working with big, strong, young horses who just don't know how to move their bodies around. Don't take it personally. It's up to you to try and get them to understand and be capable of doing what you ask.

### An alternative method
You can also try this method to get the horse to understand.

1 Stand in front but slightly to one side of your horse and press your fingertips against the base of his neck just above the chest. Consider using a training halter to make the signals a little clearer.

2 As he steps back, or in the initial stages even just leans back, release the pressure.

### MORE ADVANCED BACKING-UP EXERCISE
**Aim:** To teach a very responsive horse another method of backing up.

1 Stand about 1.2m (4ft) directly in front of your horse, holding him on a long rope. Look straight at your horse, raise your arms and take half a step towards him. If he doesn't move then just start to shake the rope from side to side in such a way that you are gradually sending more energy down the line. Couple this with the 'kiss' sound and soon the horse will take a step back, at which point you instantly stop shaking the rope.

2 When the horse is easily going back from 1.3m (4ft) away, you can gradually increase the distance between you. If your horse is in any way confused or unhappy with this, stop the exercise and continue with easier ones. It may be, again, that you just need someone to assist in teaching you the techniques or that your horse simply is not ready for this movement.

3 If your horse is very responsive and finding the exercise easy, you can even do the following exercises without touching him and with no rope. Just use your body movements and the kiss noise.

### MOVING LATERALLY EXERCISE
**Aim:** To teach horses how to move with lateral movements when being ridden. This exercise gives horses a far greater understanding of moving away from the leg, as well as having other applications, such as working around them in the stable or moving into position in the horsebox.

### CAUTION

At the beginning of this book we've emphasized that for all the work and exercises a horse must be physically sound and if there is any doubt a vet needs to be called in. The two major reasons a horse may physically not be able to back up is 'wobblers' disease, or if the horse is a 'shiverer'. This is particularly applicable to horses with shire or heavy horse blood in them. If the horse is passed sound but still seems immovable, concentrate on what you can do, for example, leading work and moving him around in circles. This will often be enough to enable him to loosen up. If it's not getting better within a couple of days, contact an expert for advice.

1 Standing along one side of your horse, keep your arm nearest his head outstretched holding his halter and with the other hand press your fingers or knuckles into his side – about where your heel would go if you were riding him. Ask him to move sideways by applying a light pressure. If he doesn't move within a couple of seconds, just bump the pressure up a fraction, making it a little more urgent. You can pair this with the verbal command 'over' as he moves, as it's useful if he understands when to step over when you're moving around him in the stable. Keep his head straight. Get him to do just one or two steps to start with and then release the pressure immediately. Give him a stroke to reassure him he's on the right track. To test how well you are doing, see whether you can get his front feet on one side of a pole and his back feet on the other side and move him laterally along the pole.

### If it's not happening

You'll find it easier if you have your horse facing a wall or fence. Another method is to 'square up' with arms outstretched along the rope. You may want to swing the rope a little if you are not getting any movement. Some horses understand more quickly if you push their hindquarters over a little and then their front end. You can progress to moving both ends at the same time. When I used to do this in my unsophisticated youth, I used to tear off a branch from a lime tree, complete with leaves, and 'tickle' the horse over. This worked very well!

BACKING-UP (SEE PAGE 64)
FROM LEFT TO RIGHT:
THE SHOW POSITION.
BACKING-UP.
MAINTAINING A
RESPECTFUL DISTANCE.

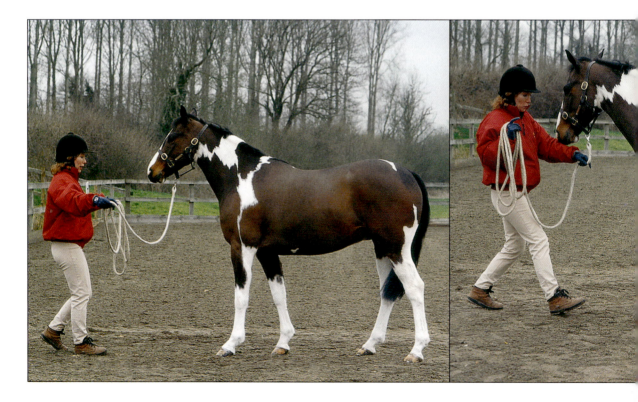

## STANDING-STILL EXERCISE

**Aim:** To get a horse to stand still.

While you may think this sounds simple enough, for some horse/rider partnerships this can be the hardest exercise of all. Any ridden horse should be able to stand still and relax as required. This is not only necessary for the show ring and competition, but it can also take the enjoyment out of 'pleasure' riding if you are on a horse that is constantly wandering around or, worse still, working himself into a lather. For some horses standing still is no problem at all – they could stand around all day. However, there is also the very active horse to be considered and as usual there is no quick-fix solution available, and absolutely no point in getting irritated or frustrated with him. It is very often our own fault, carrying our busy lives into our times with our horses. If we're always rushing somewhere with them, it's no wonder they find it hard to stand still. We've got to find a way of taking their anxiety away and getting them comfortable with the idea of standing still, even for quite long periods of time, and not consider it a hardship.

A circus act that was very popular at the turn of the century was 'living statues'. The lights would come up and the audience would see men and horses representing famous statues or paintings, maybe a war scene, the horses standing with necks arched and one foreleg raised or perhaps lying 'dead' – all absolutely motionless. This was achieved by a technique called 'modelling'. The horses were relaxed with massage and

> You have got to be able to control your horse's movement, and this means every one of your horse's feet at any time. Once you have control of your horse's feet, you pretty well have the whole horse under control too.

petting and then gradually moved and moulded into the desired position. If they moved during practice sessions they were simply put back into the position until they learned to hold it.

This 'modelling' technique is one of the ways we can get a horse to stand still: by calmly and repeatedly putting the horse back into his original position each time he moves away. It can also be used with riders. When teaching Join Up (see pages 86-107), if someone is having a problem understanding a position I'll occasionally (with permission) stand behind them with both of my hands on their shoulders and move them around so they can actually feel the position they are meant to be in. It can be an effective tool to use. But it's important to encourage the subject to take responsibility for their own movements as soon as possible. Otherwise you could find yourself holding the horse or human for longer and longer periods of time!

1 Give immediate praise when the horse stands as you would wish. Immediately correct, i.e. move back into place, when the horse moves out of the position. If the horse is very pushy and hyperactive, you may want to do a lot of backing up and coming forward again or circling as a discipline when he moves out of place. Give him the choice between being 'put to work' or standing still. Then when he starts to settle again, ask him to stand, give a sigh, and make it a 'mellow' moment to encourage him to feel, 'Ahh, standing still is just so easy.' Remember, this is for the horse's benefit. We're not attempting to turn him into a zombie that doesn't think; we are finding ways to get him to understand, and to release him from the fears and anxieties that are making him fret and fuss.

**MOVING LATERALLY
(SEE PAGE 65)
MOVING A HORSE LATERALLY
ON THE GROUND CAN GIVE
THEM A FAR GREATER
UNDERSTANDING OF MOVING
AWAY FROM THE LEG WHEN
BEING RIDDEN.**

## COMFORT-TOUCHING EXERCISE

**Aim:** To touch a horse all over. Remember, a horse must be calm to learn anything, so it's really important, as with all the exercises, to approach the horse in a relaxed, non-adversarial manner. Two lovely expressions I heard from Shiatsu practitioner Pamela Hannay are: 'You should paint the horse with your hands' and 'Every compassionate hand is a healing hand.' Touch your horse all over, including his ears, inside his mouth, tail and lower legs.

1 If you have any worries about touching a particular area, use an artificial hand (see photo on page 165) until you're happy he is relaxed enough for you to move in closer in safety. If the horse doesn't like to be touched and moves around, try and stay with him (easier with the artificial hand) and then move away the moment he stands quietly. This is your way of rewarding him: 'You see, if you stand still, I move away'.

2 A horse should stand quietly, and soon grow to enjoy greatly your stroking him all over. You can even try massage techniques as recommended by Linda Tellington-Jones or Mary Bromiley.

Your horse should allow himself to be touched all over by you. If he doesn't, ask yourself why not. You have to consider that there are issues of fear, pain, sensitivity, trust or respect that need to be faced and overcome. With any horse that comes into your care, before you even think about riding him, become aware of these problems when you first start to groom and care for him, and see what can be done to help.

When I am doing public demonstrations to show a horse accepting his first saddle and rider, within about 30 minutes I will be working with youngsters or sometimes an unrideable horse. After the Join Up, I feel all around the horse's saddle area and particularly the girth area. Sometimes you can feel the tension under there and it feels like there is almost a bulge in this area where the ganglion of nerves is so tense. Before I go on to fit the saddle and girth, I 'smooth' out that area with massaging strokes. I don't go straight on to the ticklish spot but I start just to the outside of it, where the horse is still comfortable. I then gradually go into the edge of the affected spot until I can smoothly run my hand right over the girth area and the horse remains comfortable.

To practise this exercise, find a friend with ticklish feet and give them a relaxing foot massage. You won't be able to go straight on to the soles of their feet, but if you gradually work from the outside of the feet with the right degree of pressure you will be able to get right on to the soles. Do be careful not to get kicked!

If you find uncomfortable spots along a horse's back, or in any place where you suspect it means more than just sensitivity and could be actual pain, you need to get a vet to check the horse over, and they may recommend a physiotherapist or an appropriate practitioner. When the horse is totally comfortable with this exercise, you should gradually be able to do it in larger areas with his rope hanging to the floor.

> People learn in a variety of ways and some have strong preferences as to how they take in information. Some learn through being told what to do, others through seeing what to do, while some people have to go through actually feeling the sensation. Horses are the same. A combination of two or all three of these approaches can be most effective in horse training.

## MAINTAINING A RESPECTFUL DISTANCE EXERCISE

**Aim:** To clearly and consistently move the horse back every time he steps into your space.

1 Do this by taking hold of the rope just under the halter and pushing him back immediately. This exercise is much easier to practise if you stand in front of your horse, facing towards his back end, and slightly to one side of the horse's head so that he cannot rub or push against you.

2 Once your horse becomes responsive enough (and you start to work assertively), you should find that just squaring up your shoulders, maintaining a strong eye contact and taking half a step towards him will be enough to get him to move back without further ado. Achieving this will bring a great sense of satisfactionto both you and your horse.

Remember, it is you who must consistently set the boundaries. If he has been allowed to tread all over you for the last ten years, he's going to be surprised when you suddenly change the rules. But you will find that by giving the message clearly and consistently and with positive intention the changes will soon be made. Work on raising your self-esteem (as well as that of your horse) and gaining control. Tell yourself: 'Don't you know who I am?' I'm not the sort of person that horses can tread all over!'

**'L' FOR LEATHER**

THIS EXERCISE IS VERY USEFUL TO SUPPLE YOUR HORSE AND TO TEACH YOU HOW TO CONTROL YOUR HORSE'S DIRECTION.

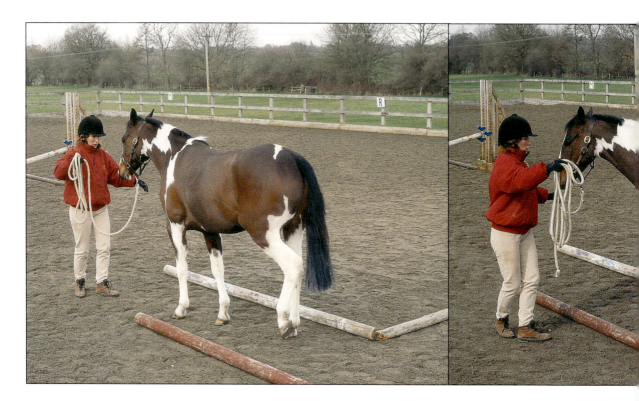

## THE 'L' FOR LEATHER EXERCISE

**Aim:** To get the horse to back through poles set in an 'L' shape.

This exercise is a deceptively simple one, and the benefits go much further than just enabling you to manoeuvre your horse. It's also an exercise in responsiveness and trust. Here you set poles out to make a hollow figure 'L' as shown in the photographs below – this only involves four poles.

1 Back your horse through the poles, keeping within the 'L' shape. It seems simple, and yet hardly any new horse that comes to our yard can complete it when they first arrive. It's not just the horses but the owners as well who find it really hard initially to work out how they should position themselves. Perhaps it's a little like reversing a trailer for humans – to start with you are inclined to go in the opposite direction to the one you should go in.

2 To make life easier for both of you, start with the poles set really far apart and work your way forwards through the poles. Walking backwards yourself, keep a short but very light hold on the rope, so you can communicate your wishes quickly to the horse. Ask the horse to take only one or two steps at a time, so that you can really check that he is paying full attention to you. You can teach the horse to stop when you raise your hands, which will further help establish where your personal

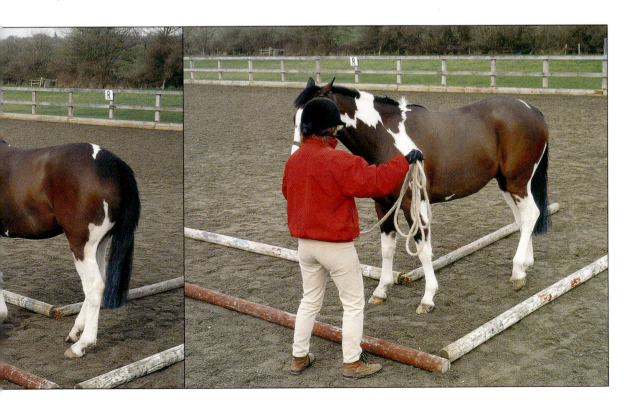

space starts – about an arm's length. Come through the 'L' shape several times in this way, until you can get through confidently with the horse positioned exactly where you want him. Then it's time to think backwards!

3 To make sure that you position yourself correctly for the backwards movement, break it down into small parts. Start by asking your horse to move forwards into the 'L' a few steps, and then back him out again. I think of this exercise being like 'oiling the wheels' – as you keep working, the horse becomes looser and more yielding moment by moment.

4 Repeat until you reach the corner of the 'L'. Keep moving forwards a step or two and then backwards until you've worked out how to negotiate the turn. As long as you take one step at a time, and the horse doesn't rush, you can work out how to move his feet. If it seems too difficult, make the shape a bit wider. Remember, you can move him forwards, backwards and sideways using the techniques described.

## STANDING IN THE CORRECT POSITION

With a little attention it is not difficult to get a horse to stand in the correct 'show' or photograph position – all four legs should be visible from the near side, the near fore should be placed to the front.

Initially, you may like to use one of the training halters to give you a little added finesse and to ensure you can correctly place each one of his feet.

This is one of those common problems that occur because people don't consider it something they should work on with their horse – they think the horse should somehow know to stand still and in a certain way. They don't, it's something that needs to be worked on.

If it's something you want to improve, go out and dedicate 10 minutes a day to this exercise with your horse. Make sure your horse enjoys these sessions as well though, by giving him plenty of reward and fuss when he's getting it right.

5 If the horse tries to rush out, or accidentally steps across the poles, just calmly start again at the beinning. Try to keep relaxed and make sure your requests are completely clear and unambiguous at all times. Sometimes horses will be reluctant to take a step back if they think they're about to hit a pole, so just be calmly insistent. If you do accidentally cause your horse to tap a pole, just apologise and then carry on with the practice session.

6 Repeat the exercise slowly moving the poles nearer each other until you can move the horse through a narrow 'L'. But don't make any one session too long – about 15 minutes is ideal. Keep an eye on your horse's expression – he should have his ears at 'half mast' in concentration. If he starts looking miserable, call it a day. It's meant to be interesting for him, not a trial.

This exercise teaches humans to think about how horses move and learn the concept of (literally) taking one step at a time. It is a wonderful exercise for horses because it really teaches them two things in particular: first to concentrate hard on where and how they are placing their feet (relevant in so many of these 'manners' problems); and second, to help them to become more supple, learning to bend, but as we ask them to – not against us. In some ways, horses' minds seem to be very much connected to their feet.

It requires time, patience and focused thought for you both to perform this exercise easily but it is most definitely worth the effort. Complete these exercises and fill in the checklist below to see what progress you are making before trying others in the book.

## CHECKLIST

I now have (HORSE'S NAME).........................................................................................

1 Is happy to be touched all over with no resistance

DATE ...................................................................................................................

2 Coming smoothly towards you off a long line of 3m (10ft) in a straight line

DATE ...................................................................................................................

3 Backing up easily, including one step at a time

DATE ...................................................................................................................

4 Moving over sideways smoothly and easily from either side, including over a pole

DATE ...................................................................................................................

5 Standing still as requested for

DATE ........................................................................................... 1 minutes

DATE ........................................................................................... 3 minutes

DATE ........................................................................................... 4 minutes

6 Doing the exercise 'L for Leather', including one step at a time and bending in either direction quite easily

DATE ...................................................................................................................

# *additional yielding* EXERCISES

These are a few simple exercises used by Western trainers to check that their horses are really yielding to pressure with no resistance – again serving to 'oil all the wheels', as it were. These exercises, as well as increasing suppleness and lightness, are also an opportunity to build up mutual trust with your horse and increase understanding and communication. I have found working with horses on the ground is an excellent way to see how they work things out, to see their responses, and consequently to really get to know them.

These exercises are useful in addition to the Foundation Exercises (see previous chapter), which you are advised to do first. They will all be of help to training a new horse, whether a youngster, or one with remedial problems. Once the horse finds them easy, they can be used after that for the odd change in routine, or if it's felt there is some resistance that could be helped with the exercises. Please understand: there is no need to drill your horse with these exercises. What we want is a contented, supple, willing horse – not an automaton.

## FOCUS

Sometimes these exercises can be good just to bring the horse's focus and attention back on the handler before proceeding to other areas. However, the majority of cases of lack of concentration in horses is caused by overexcitement and freshness. If you can turn your horse out in a round pen for half an hour before you start a training session, it will often make your life easier. Don't make the choice to fight against his natural impulses but wait until he has settled down and is ready to concentrate. Boredom is another enemy of attention. Make sure that once your horse has reached the stage of finding the exercises easy that you don't drill him to distraction with them. Remember, we can use 'boredom training' (aka 'habituation') with excellent results in some of our training of horses – for example, to get the previously nervous horse to

HEAD-LOWERING
(SEE OVERLEAF)
ONE WAY TO ENCOURAGE YOUR HORSE TO LOWER HIS HEAD IS TO REST YOUR HAND GENTLY BUT FIRMLY ON HIS POLL, RELEASING THE PRESSURE AS SOON AS HE RELAXES.

side with the hand on the nose to gently ease him into relaxing. Remember to remove your hands to reward the slightest sign of lowering the head.

2 If he moves his body around, just stay with him quietly. Don't make it a problem and make him feel trapped or restricted. Move your feet in time with his. If he has successfully completed the Foundation Exercises you should find that he will soon settle down to this exercise as well. You should reach the stage where you can not only lower the horse's head on request but also touch it all over while you are squatting down.

### NECK FLEXING EXERCISE

**Aim:** To gently ease any resistance in the head and neck area in order to help avoid problems when you are on the ground and when you are riding the horse.

1 Put one hand on the bridge of the horse's nose, at least a hand's width above the nostrils, and the other on top of his neck, about a hand's width behind his poll.

2 Gently flex his head laterally in the area where his head meets his neck. As with all exercises, do this from both sides.

**FOLLOWING PRESSURE**
YOUR HORSE CAN LEARN TO WORK OUT HOW TO FOLLOW THE DIRECTION FROM THE PRESSURE THAT IS APPLIED.

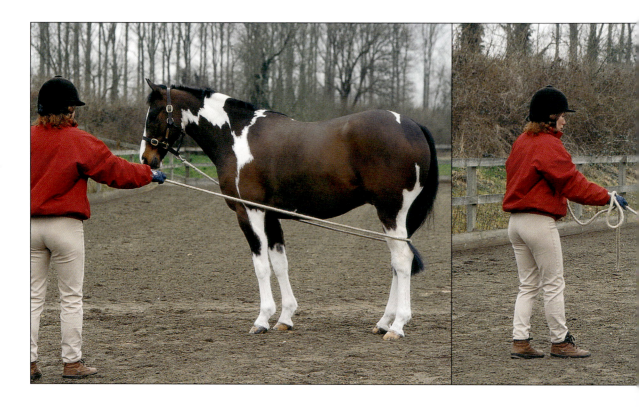

## If it's not happening

If your horse resists with his head, just gently persist. This should be a pleasurable experience for him, so continue in a similar way as if you were just petting and relaxing him. If he keeps moving his hindquarters round to get away, try working first of all by a wall or fence, making sure he doesn't feel trapped in any way, but just helping him to understand that the answer is to comply with the movement of your hand.

## FOLLOWING PRESSURE EXERCISE

**Aim:** To teach the horse to follow pressure even when he can't see where it's coming from, as well as encouraging suppleness and a feeling of calm.

1 Standing by your horse's neck, put the rope under it and pass it to your other hand at the top of his neck, then gently let the rope fall along the far side of your horse's body – at the back end it should fall just above his hocks as it comes along his body back up to you.

## If it's not happening

1 He's frightened of the rope. If at any stage your horse seems concerned, rather than push on and 'spook' him, stop the exercises and work on more touching exercises with him, this time using the rope. You can start by just draping the rope over his body from the side you are

> **WARNING**
>
> Never wrap a rope around your hand or fingers – it's a good way to lose a finger.

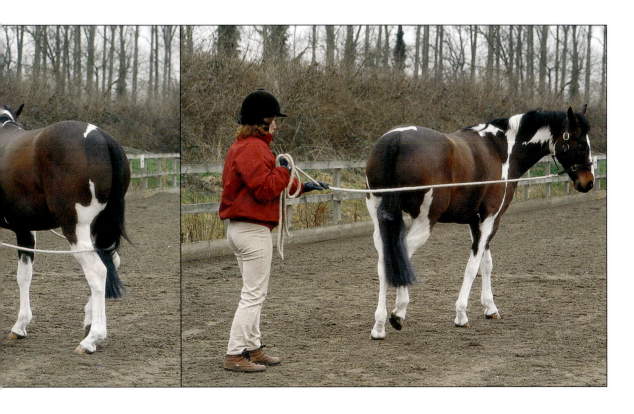

on, and when he is comfortable with that, start hanging the rope over his back and then right down the other side of his body.

2 He's frightened of the rope tightening over his hocks. This can also happen when you first go to long-line a youngster. Remember that with the Foundation Exercises (see previous chapter) you have already checked whether you can touch the horse all over. You can also test with the artificial 'hand' to touch above his hocks. However, if you're not sure how your horse will react you should take the same precautions that I do before long-lining. If you lack confidence or experience, this may be a job where you want professional help to start with, so that you can see exactly what is expected of you.

What I do to test just how the horse is going to react with the rope over his hocks is to work with two 4.5m (15ft) ropes. If I am working from the nearside, I clip one line on the outside of his headcollar on the nearside and feed the other rope over his neck and then coming under his neck clip it on the outside of the headcollar on the offside. Holding the horse on just a foot or two of line, I encourage him to stand next to me in a relaxed fashion and gently let the offside rope slip along the other side of his body. I deliberately slide it along, 'toing and froing' it on his back to test his reactions. If the horse fusses as he's going round, I just stay on the same spot. As he gradually settles I'll go further back with it – to 'test the water' as it were.

As he seems to get more relaxed, you can gently let it drop over his tail and on to his hocks. If he darts forward just hold him and let him go round you for a few circles. You are in a safe position and he's not going anywhere. He'll very likely stop himself after two or three rounds when he sees the rope's staying with him. When he does, make a big fuss of him, tell him how brave he is and after a minute or two ask him to move on again. He will relax with the rope in a few minutes, generally. The horse that is far trickier is the one that kicks out violently at the rope so that you can't hold it.

Remember, you shouldn't be in any danger of getting kicked because you are holding his head towards you, just to the side, so you won't get run over. It can be impossible to hold the rope if a horse does a really good kick, and when you feel the power of some kicks you know you are really better off not holding on – it will do a lot of damage to you if you are still attached to the rope. Work at holding the rope higher so the horse can't get to kick it, but if the horse kicks the rope right out of you hand it's not the end of the world (or the training session).

It may be that you want to do some work with your artificial hand, gently stroking the back of his hocks. If he kicks out you'll still be able to keep hold of the hand and replace it immediately. Supposing he's all right with the hand but still hates the rope? Become innovative! How can you safely dangle some rope over his hocks? Get used to thinking up solutions yourself. Once you're sure you've covered all eventualities go back to feeding the rope over his back and start again with the steps outlined on the previous page. Hold the rope a little higher to start with. He'll eventually understand the rope over his hocks isn't going to harm him and you can do your long-lining or yielding exercises, if not on this day, then as soon as you feel he's ready.

3 He can't figure out how to follow the pressure from the rope. If this is the case, just help him out a bit. In the early stages you need to teach him what it is you want him to do. It's not a test that he either passes or fails. Make it easy for him to understand. Maybe push his head away from you or move a little more to the back of him to make it as easier for him to understand as possible. Once he has that 'lightbulb' moment, he'll then find it easy and it shouldn't be a problem again.

## DISENGAGING HINDQUARTERS EXERCISE

**Aim:** In this exercise the horse moves his hindquarters around his forehand. The forelegs move forward in a smaller circle, and the hindlegs take bigger steps, crossing under the horse's body. (Note: This is slightly different to the dressage movement 'turn about the forehand', in that the forelegs don't stay still, but is a useful starting point for that exercise.) As well as making the horse more supple, this exercise will help him to manoeuvre better through gates and doorways. When transferred to ridden work it can be a very useful way of ending forward movement – useful on a fresh horse out hacking, for example, or a horse that is starting to bolt.

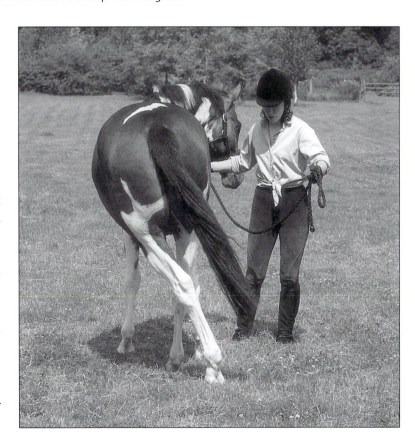

1 From the nearside, stand by your horse facing his hindquarters. Put your left hand on the halter rope a couple of feet from his jaw, holding the slack in your right hand. Move towards his hindquarters, using clear body language and jerky movements. Do this positively and it will encourage your horse to move correctly.

DISENGAGING HINDQUARTERS THE NEAREST HINDLEG SHOULD GO INSIDE THE OUTSIDE HINDLEG AS THE HORSE MOVES AROUND.

2 Give a little tug on the rope to encourage his head to come towards you and for him to take the first step. If necessary twirl the end of the rope towards his hindquarters – not to touch him with it, nor to intimidate him, but just to make your request clearer.

3 As soon as he moves his hindlegs away, reward him. Let him stop, give him a rub, and then try again. Your aim is to get him moving smoothly in a circle, with his hindlegs moving in a wide arc around his front legs, which continue on a smaller circle, but to start with praise him for any attempt that looks anything like this movement.

**If it's not happening**

It may be worth trying from the other side, as he may be particularly stiff in one direction, or find it impossible to cross his legs under his body. If he can do it in one direction and not the other, and doesn't seem to be improving after a few attempts, it's worth getting him looked at by a vet or professional equine body worker. Used carefully, these exercises can help alleviate stiffness, and make the horse less one-sided, but they will obviously not cure a serious physiological problem.

If he finds it difficult in both directions, and doesn't seem to understand the request to move away, try tapping the side of his flank with the fingers of your right hand (when working from the nearside), to encourage him to move away. Make sure you bring his head around towards you at the same time, to prevent him simply moving laterally away from you.

Only use an occasional tugging or 'bumping' movement on the headcollar. Too strong or continuous a pull can cause him to move his forehand over towards you too much, stifling the action of the back legs.

Repeat this exercise from both sides until your horse understands fully and is moving freely in both directions. Remember to keep each session short, and make sure your horse is not becoming bored or irritated by the work.

## MOVING THE FOREHAND AROUND THE HINDQUARTERS EXERCISE

**Aim:** This is the mirror image of the previous exercise, and is also useful for manoeuvrability. It can help lighten the forehand and increase suppleness.

In this exercise, the horse moves his forelegs in a large circle around his hindquarters, which should remain still. Unlike the standard dressage pirouette, backward movement is preferred over forward movement, as it helps the horse take the weight on his haunches, whereas forward movement tends to drop the weight on to the horse's forehand.

**1** A horse that understands the basic principles of moving away and out of your space when asked will find this exercise quite easy to work out. Stand about halfway along your horse's neck, facing his head. If starting from the nearside, use your left hand to hold the rope a foot or so from his nose, and take up the slack in your right hand. If you are starting from the farside, reverse your hands.

**2** Move purposefully towards his head, looking him in the eye with your shoulders square and the rope held high in your hands. Make a kissing noise to encourage movement. Your horse should start to move his front end away from you. Don't be too concerned about his exact positioning to start with, just reward every try. Work from both sides, increasing the number of steps that he takes, until the horse is fluent in both directions.

### If it's not happening

**1** If your horse moves backwards, you're standing too close to his head. If he moves forwards, you're standing too close to his shoulder. Adjust your position accordingly. If he tries to dash off, you're probably using too strong a signal. Don't reprimand him for trying to leave, simply bring him back to you, and start again, using a more

WALK ON (SEE OVERLEAF) TEACHING YOUR HORSE TO WALK IN FRONT OF YOU HAS QUITE A FEW USES IN EVERYDAY LIFE.

# the art of
# JOIN UP

Before we deal with any specific problems a horse may have, we first need to establish trust, respect and create a bond with the horse. The process that Monty Roberts calls 'Join Up' can be a wonderful aid to these requirements and I use it, when possible and whenever appropriate, with many horses I'm asked to help. By communicating with the horse in his own language I can often make a major breakthrough in his attitude towards me and, in fact, his attitude to all humans. Once a horse has achieved Join Up with one human being he will transfer that to all humans. However, that is not to say the spell can't be broken if the horse is treated unkindly in the future.

I should perhaps be cautious about using the word 'spell'. I hate to ever infer that there are miracles available in horse training. However, just occasionally, I must admit, this process does appear to bring about a miracle. It's like the horse is saying, 'At last. What I have waited for all my life – a human being that actually speaks my language!'

Join Up is the art of getting a horse to want to be with you and choose to stay with you as you walk around. Some people say that their horse is already Joined Up because he follows them around. This might not be technically correct because it was Monty Roberts that coined the phrase and he specifically means Join Up to apply to the process I'll describe. However, it may mean the horse has a really good bond with people already, and if the rest of your relationship is going exactly as you'd like, that's wonderful.

## HOW TO DO JOIN UP WITH YOUR HORSE

The following is a step-by-step guide to the Join Up process. This is a very specific procedure where you take a halter-broken young horse into an arena to work using just body language. I would advise you are sure your horse can do all the Foundation Exercises (see earlier chapter) easily first. This will make your Join Up much easier and stress-free.

FIRST THINGS FIRST BEFORE DOING ANYTHING ELSE YOU FIRST NEED TO ESTABLISH TRUST AND RESPECT AND CREATE A BOND WITH YOUR HORSE.

*Case study*

# TRUST IS FOR LIFE, NOT JUST FOR CHRISTMAS

*I remember using the Join Up system, possibly for only the second or third time, with a nervous young racehorse filly we called Lucy. As I went in to do the Join Up I was slightly horrified to see a crowd of about 20 visitors to the yard gathering to watch, curious to know what this was all about. It made me hesitant and a little unsure in places but Lucy went through the process as though she'd read a book on it.*

*Every sign was in place, she followed me around devotedly and, although clearly apprehensive, accepted her first saddle and later her rider with a touching amount of trust. There wasn't a dry eye in the crowd! She was a great little racehorse and went on to win two races in her first season. When photographs were quickly needed to show Join Up for Monty Roberts' book* The Man Who Listens to Horses *I brought Lucy out because I knew she'd be one of the few horses in a yard of racehorses (I hadn't worked with the others) that would be prepared to have a photographer actually in the round pen with her, and who would not be worried or lose her concentration on the handler. I was away helping Monty on his demonstration book tour when I heard that Lucy had very bad colic. I got home very late at night and stayed most of the night in her box. By 4am things were taking a turn for the worse; the vet came out again and said keeping her alive now was only prolonging her pain.*

*I'm only telling the story to remind us all that owning a horse is a great responsibility. There is so much pleasure to be had, but also some very hard decisions to be taken. I led her outside in the rain that morning – she was the first horse I had to hold for the vet to put to sleep. This is a horrible experience which I hope you never have to go through. What we have to remember, though, is that when we took horses out of the wild, we also took predators out of their life. If a horse in the wild is injured in any way, he doesn't have to suffer very long because a predator will be somewhere close to end his misery. With all the good things that we get from horse ownership we also have to take on that awesome responsibility – the decision when to end a horse's life. Having a horse gives us so much. Our responsibility to them doesn't finish – right up to the last moment of their life.*

## STEP 1 – FIND A SUITABLE ENCLOSURE

1 Join Up can be performed in any safe area, although the easiest place to do this is generally a custom-built round pen about 15m (50ft) in diameter. It is not essential, however, and, a school or manège are perfectly adequate – you can block off corners if you are worried about a horse getting 'stuck' in them. A large area can be made smaller by putting up jump wings and poles.

2 It is possible to make a round pen out of electric fencing (switched off, of course) taped in a circle. Use your imagination, but make sure that if you do use any of these less conventional enclosures that

the horse would end up somewhere safe if he did jump out – into another field, not on to a road.

## STEP 2 – SENDING THE HORSE AWAY

It is central to the Join Up process that the horse understands that you can send him away; that he understands you can direct his movement just as a more dominant horse would in the herd. Just as Eskimoes are reputed to have 94 different words to describe snow, so you will gradually learn that there is far more to 'sending away' than just chasing after a horse. These subtleties should apply to every aspect of our horsemanship. There is no need to shout all the time – if you do you will never hear the response. I'm going to describe here the main approaches to getting the horse to move away from you.

1 Sending the horse away starts as you lead the horse into the enclosure on your long line and you unclip him, letting him loose and waiting until he starts to move off of his own accord. When he does, you adopt the more aggressive body language, effectively saying, 'OK, if you want to go away go right away.'

2 The second approach is to be more proactive in asking the horse to go away. As you unclip, immediately look your horse hard in the eye. Back off slowly but with your body positioning square at his head and holding the line between your outstretched arms. Move your arms alternately up and down and gradually work yourself to the back of the horse (avoiding the kick zone).

3 As you reach the back of the horse you are justified in gently throwing the long line at him.

---

### KEY POINTS TO SENDING THE HORSE AWAY

• Direct eye contact.

• Shoulders square.

• Standing at 45 degrees behind the horse.

• Jerky movements.

• Making yourself big.

---

### NEW TO JOIN UP

On the courses I run in Oxfordshire we receive a constant stream of horses and work with a great deal that haven't done Join Up before. However, we also have three or four 'schoolmaster' horses that have been through the process a fair few times. They will wait quietly while the student unclips them but as soon as the student starts the second technique as described, with eye contact and outstretched arms, they understand straight away and move off around the pen.

Using clear procedures at all times helps to prevent misunderstandings between you and the horse. You certainly don't want the horse to think that every time you unclip him he is expected to run away.

JOINING UP (OVERLEAF)
TAKE IT SLOWLY AND STEP BY
STEP AND SOON YOU AND YOUR
HORSE WILL FORM A DEEP AND
LASTING BOND.

4 Keep the horse moving away from you at a brisk trot or steady canter for about five to six circuits of the pen. He should be moving on respectfully, but not in fear of you. If he is just jogging along, he may not be taking you very seriously. Holding out your outside hand with the fingers spread out is often perceived as an aggressive gesture and encourages the horse to go faster. You may need to throw the line behind him and make your moving more aggressive and jerky. Walk in a larger circle so you can be more behind him. Sometimes hitting yourself with the coil line is an effective way of moving the horse on. If he is moving too fast you are probably putting on too much pressure. Don't throw the line but just hold it out behind him. Walk slowly in a smaller circle. Be sure you are reaching a happy medium.

### STEP 3 – CHANGING THE HORSE'S DIRECTION

It is an important part of the process to change the horse's direction, indicating to him that you are in charge of his direction as well as his speed. Also, the horse needs to see you with both eyes and get used to you going out of view and coming back into view.

1 To change the horse's direction, you need to block the horse's forward movement by moving in front of him. This effectively closes off one part of the pen and opens up another. If the horse is cantering, you will need to cut straight across the pen to get in front of him. If he

**STAGES OF JOIN UP**

**FROM LEFT TO RIGHT:**

**SENDING AWAY.**

**CHANGING DIRECTION.**

**THE HORSE GRADUALLY**

**STARTING TO LOWER HIS HEAD.**

is trotting about a third of the pen will be sufficient. Be sure to maintain eye contact and aggressive body language throughout.

2 Allow the horse to explore the new direction, again for about five or six circuits and then turn him back to his original 'flight' path. By now, in a 15m (50ft) round pen, the horse will have travelled approximately 0.5km (¼ mile). This is the average 'run' of any predator that would be chasing him in the wild. By now the horse will either have got clean away or be taken as dinner. Be clear that we are not imitating a predator in this process but we are using our knowledge of how horses interact with each other. However, it's still interesting to note that, perhaps because of this predator/prey process that is inherently in their mind, after about a quarter of a mile some horse will often start giving clear signals to 'renegotiate the deal'.

Please note that using this body language in addition to the line is an art that gets better with practice. We always encourage students to practise these things on each other before they are let loose on a horse.

### STEP 4 – INVITING THE HORSE IN

1 Our aim now is for the horse to make the decision that he wants to be with us. We don't just drop the pressure, but we work to make the process as smooth as possible to make it easy and clear for the horse

### CAUTION

Do remember this is not a test for your horse to pass or fail. This interaction can be the starting point for you to learn a lot more about your horse and to give you insight into the correct way to proceed.

to come right in to us. Before you even think about inviting the horse in you need to make sure your line is fully coiled up. Think in advance where would be a good place to invite the horse in. Asking the horse to move from the gate is not advisable, or even from a part of the pen where there are any distractions. The area where the horse has given the most signals is often a good place to start. Drop your eyes down the horse's body a little and you may note him looking towards you a little more. When you have reached the spot you intended and feel the moment is right, you can drop your eye contact altogether and move gently away from the horse, ending up at a position of 45 degrees in front of him, where he can easily see you. Adopt passive body language, rounding your shoulders slightly and turning your body so the horse can see you side on.

2 Keep still and give the horse the chance to walk up to you, or at least look in your direction and evaluate how the situation has changed. Although, you have dropped your eye contact and are facing away from the horse, you should still be able to see him in your peripheral vision, i.e. just out of the corner of your eye.

3 If the horse comes right up to you, that's wonderful, but if he just stands and faces you and doesn't move, don't worry – we have a plan 'b' as well as a 'c' and 'd'. You can encourage steps towards you by

**JOIN UP CONTINUED**
FROM LEFT TO RIGHT:
INVITING THE HORSE IN.
COMING TOWARDS YOU.
FOLLOW UP.

moving in semicircles and arcs around the horse's head. Just a few steps and then wait for a few seconds. Gauge your horse's reaction. Is he paying you attention? Turn round, look him briefly in the eye to check you still have his attention and take a few steps in the other direction.

4 Bring each semicircle a little closer to him. If he starts walking towards you, wait for him; at the very least, if you keep walking make sure it's away because if you walk towards him you will stop him moving immediately. What you are trying to achieve now is for the horse to take even just a couple of steps voluntarily towards you. He may even reach out with his nose to your shoulders to confirm the Join Up. If he doesn't, it may be because he is insecure. It's good that you understand this and you now know you need to work on his confidence. Keep circling until you get close to him, and then give him a reassuring rub between the eyes, if the horse will accept this.

## FOLLOW UP

1 When you are near his head, give him a lovely rub between the eyes and then walk away moving in circles (see photograph below). Start by circling on the right hand, and make the diameter of the circle about the same distance as the length of the horse. Walk in a smooth, workmanlike fashion. Once one direction is accomplished you can reward the horse with a rub and then circle in the opposite direction. Most horses

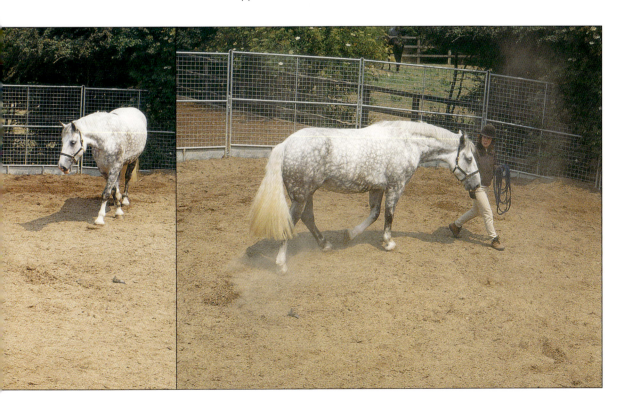

seem to find it easier to go to the right so we generally go in that direction first. If you stand on the nearside or left-hand side getting him to move to the right can be easy because you are walking slightly into him.

2 You may find it easier to stand on the offside (right-hand side) to go round to the left. When you have achieved the second direction be sure to reward him again with a lovely rub. He should follow you in both directions or at least move to maintain his head in your direction. If he finds it a little difficult at first, as an insecure horse might, you can give the headcollar a little 'prompt'. Just very lightly lay a hand on the outside of the headcollar and bring him with you a couple of strides before letting go of the headcollar, without hesitating in your walk.

If you can achieve this follow up it means that the horse has started to understand you are his safety zone, that things are easy and pleasant for him near you, and if he is frightened or confused this is the place to be. The effects of this can be profound for both of you. I have seen horses totally change their whole attitude after this process, in effect saying – 'At last, somebody who understands me.'

## SIGNS OF JOIN UP

As the horse is going round we are looking for signals from him to show us he would like to Join Up.

### EAR LOCKED ON

When the horse turns his inside ear towards you, it's a clear sign that he is giving you his attention. He is aware that you are worthy of attention and so, in this way, is showing you respect as well. Meanwhile, the outside ear may be pointing to the outside of the pen, figuring out what's happening out there. This is usually the first sign you will observe, often very soon after you send the horse away.

### MAKING THE CIRCLE SMALLER

When the horse makes the circle smaller, it shows that he wants to come in to you. He understands that it is better to be close to you. Just be sure it isn't an aversion to the pen wall that is making him want to come closer in, though, and also that he has genuinely agreed to go away in the first place. For this reason it is always a good idea to let your horse acclimatize to the pen for a little while first. Making the circle smaller at the start of the process may have a different meaning to making the circle smaller towards the end.

### LOWERING THE HEAD

This may be a dramatic gesture, with the head bobbing along the ground, or a more subtle gesture, with the horse just relaxing his head slightly. This is a submissive gesture, similar to a person bowing or with their hands up, or a dog lying on his back. It's making the horse very vulnerable; in a way he is saying that he is giving us trust. It is not a signal you could or should force; on the contrary, it's a gesture that needs to be invited.

What greatly assists achieving this response is to let up the pressure in the area of the pen where the horse shows any sign of this gesture; for instance, look closely for the slightest dip or relaxation of the neck. He will tend to do this on the same spot where he feels most comfortable on each circuit. When he gets to this spot, keep him moving but don't throw the line at all, or put any additional pressure on. If you're back on the right path but still haven't had the lowering of the head at this spot, you can try letting your horse really relax, and although you keep him going round, you can let him even walk for a stride or two to see if that encourages his head to drop.

## LICKING AND CHEWING

A horse will sometimes lick and chew as he goes round the pen, in particular the first time you ever do this process with him. This is a throwback to what the foal does with his mother and more dominant members of the herd. This is generally a submissive gesture indicating, 'I'm just a little baby. I don't mean any harm.' Many times when a horse is even the slightest bit anxious you will see him lick and chew. In fact, you will often see this same trait in humans beings who are anxious. Again, clearly this is not a signal you want to force; it is more something just to note. Is this horse anxious and very submissive? Or is he accepting being sent round the pen with equanimity? If you don't see any licking and chewing but, taking everything else into account, still feel it's the right time to invite him in, it is likely that he will lick and chew as he walks towards you. This is just as respectful and valid and, in fact, far more common in a horse that has been round the pen before, even if only briefly. (See also Displacement in Behaviourism for Beginners, page 215.)

*He who binds to himself a Joy*
*Does the winged life destroy;*
*But he who kisses the Joy as it flies*
*Lives in Eternity's sunrise*

WILLIAM BLAKE

Experience coupled with paying attention will sharpen your senses to communicating with your horse. The clearer you are in your communication, the easier it is for your horse to be clear with you. If you don't feel it has gone as you would like, don't push the horse on too long, demanding signals. I suggest that whether you get signals or not, you don't go on any longer than six minutes unless you are under expert supervision.

Remember this is not a test for your horse to pass or fail. Instead, think of this interaction as the starting point for you to learn a lot more about your horse and to try to discover the correct way to proceed that will suit you both.

## WHAT TO DO IF IT'S NOT HAPPENING
### 'MY HORSE WON'T GO AWAY'

I find that the most common human errors for horses not going away are inconsistent eye contact and not being at the right angle behind the horse to send him away successfully. Also a strong 'intention' is necessary; you need to go out there and project your energy as a truly powerful person.

**TOUCHING ALL OVER**

GENTLY PAINT THE HORSE WITH YOUR HANDS.

1 To be sure you are using consistent eye contact, count how many times the horse blinks as he goes round.

2 Make sure you are a suitable distance behind the horse and at a 45-degree angle. Getting too close to the front of the horse will effectively block him and slow down his energy.

3 Throw the line out at him, making sure you are keeping your eyes hard on his eyes and not getting distracted and looking at where the end of the line is going. You can whizz the line in a circle so it goes round like a windmill. You can also fold the line up and slap it across your chest (particularly effective if you are wearing some sort of water-proof clothing – not so good in a T-shirt). You can raise your arms together or, alternatively, stamp your feet; sometimes squeaky or kissing noises can help.

4 If you are sure it isn't you being ineffective, it may be that the horse has been overhandled as a foal or perhaps you have been through the procedure too many times. If you are using a strong energy but the horse isn't going away, and in a worse-case scenario is just standing there and even kicking out, it's time to think again. Look at the Alternative to Join Up method (see page 101) or put a roller on with your horse and then get him moving on long lines. Your horse is not necessarily stubborn but may be insecure and need his confidence building with leading work for a while. Do not consider inflicting pain as a way to move him away; this would defeat the whole object.

## 'MY HORSE KEEPS CHANGING DIRECTION'

This usually happens when you get too far in front of the horse, blocking the space he was about to go into. As far as he's concerned, you are asking him to change direction. It's a common fault among students, in their enthusiasm to keep the horse moving, to 'race' the horse at the change of direction, and inadvertently send him back the other way.

1 Remember, he's looking for a clear space to move into. So give him that space. Sometimes the change in direction happens because he is being distracted by something outside the pen.

2 If it keeps happening in the same spot, make sure you anticipate this and put a little more pressure on before he gets to that area.

## 'MY HORSE DOESN'T FOLLOW ME'

Make sure the circles are of the right size; their diameter should be about the same as the length of the horse's body. Too small a circle and the horse finds it more difficult to follow as he has to bend round on himself and may think you are just walking down the side of his body. Too large a circle initially, doesn't draw the horse with you as well.

1 Make sure you are walking confidently as a healthy confident person would. A common student mistake is to walk too tentatively or too slowly, which sends the signal 'Oh please, please follow me!' This doesn't encourage the horse at all. It's not natural for horses to walk that slowly. Like us, they want confidence from the person they are following and a feeling that the person knows where they are going. If the horse hasn't come round to you by the time you have got level with his hip bone, you could stop and shuffle your feet a little bit, or make the kiss noise, just to be sure his attention is on you.

2 If that doesn't help and he clearly doesn't understand, you can try going back, giving him a rub and bringing him on the headcollar for a stride or two. If he wanders off when you are doing follow up, once you are right behind him (keeping out of the kick zone) you can put him back to work for three or four circuits and then invite him in again. This can work well in making the options clearer to the horse but mustn't be overused. I'd always encourage people to take the attitude that it's their fault if the horse isn't joining up and following up, rather than encouraging them to blame the horse and keep putting him back to work.

As I said, if you take this option once, at a push twice, it can have the desired effect, but any more times than that can get into a negative spiral, with the horse not understanding where he's meant to be. We want the horse to choose to be with us; if he's clearly not understanding or for some reason isn't choosing to take that option, we need to examine the situation carefully. We need to check that we have done all the preliminary exercises thoroughly and that our body language and attitude are just as they should be. Rather than let a session go on too long, if the follow up isn't going exactly as you'd like, I'd suggest you just clip a lead rope on the horse and walk round on the loosest line with him, tell him how good he is and then think how possibly you could improve things or work differently at another training session.

### 'MY HORSE WON'T TURN IN OR MAKE THE CIRCLE SMALLER. HE SEEMS IN A TRANCE AND JUST RUNS AROUND NOT SEEING ME'

Has your horse ever been lunged? Cutting in or turning to look at you are both generally reprimanded on the lunge. Horses which have been lunged extensively, with the trainer standing in the middle of the circle, have had to learn to ignore the body-language signals being given to them, and therefore often 'switch off'. Changing the horse's direction several times can help focus attention. You may have to stand passively for even a minute when inviting in, until the horse really 'gets the message'.

## 'MY HORSE IS TOO DISTRACTED'

If you want to do a Join Up with a horse and he keeps calling to his companions, turn him out in the round pen for 20 minutes to an hour and let him settle down before you start. It is much easier if he can't see other horses, particularly those ones that are distracting him. However, it is possible he will still be distracted, and you just need to work harder to keep his attention.

## 'THERE'S GRASS IN THE ROUND PEN AND MY PONY JUST WANTS TO KEEP EATING IT'

I know this one! This is making life far too difficult for yourself and it's unfair on your horse or pony (ponies find it particularly hard to resist) to have this great temptation. Let him have some turnout time there at some stage and rid the area of as much grass as possible. A permanent (non-edible) surface is better, if at all possible.

## 'I DON'T HAVE ANYTHING I CAN USE AS A ROUND PEN' OR 'IT'S JUST NOT WORKING FOR ME"

Remember the primary purpose of Join Up is to establish yourself as a comfort zone, a pleasant place to be, and to illustrate to your horse that you can communicate using body language. Ideally, it's best if your horse can have complete freedom at the time so that you really are 'speaking with him in his own language'. However, if your horse is confused by your methods of communication, it may be worth considering an alternative way of achieving at least some 'connection', until you can get some good lessons in body language. It's important when doing Join Up that you don't confuse the horse. (Actually it's a good idea generally, to try not to confuse your horse.) If you've had a couple of attempts at Join Up and you don't feel you're getting anywhere, I have an alternative technique that can be helpful. It's also useful if you don't have suitable facilities – for example, your arena isn't fenced, or you're working in a large open space – or for whatever reason you feel an alternative may be a good idea.

## AN ALTERNATIVE TO JOIN UP

1 Instead of having your horse loose, attach a long line, about 3.6m (12ft), to his headcollar, look him in the eye with a positive intention and, giving him about 1.8m (6ft) of line initially, send him in a circle around you. This isn't the same as conventional lunging, because you'll be positioning yourself at an angle of 45 degrees behind him. You can throw the end of the line towards his hocks to encourage forward

### CAUTION

Do not overdo these exercises – they can cause too much 'wear and tear' on your horse.

movement, and continue with the same assertive body language as when sending the horse away. If you accidentally get a little ahead of him, and he thinks you want him to change direction, and starts doing so, step back to your correct position, and just put a little pressure on his head to keep him in his original direction.

2 Keep the horse trotting long enough to establish a rhythm – four or five circuits is plenty – and then ask him in to you by dropping your eyes, taking a step backwards and putting a little pressure on the rope if necessary. Once the horse has come to you, give him a lovely rub and indicate that is just what you wanted him to do. You can then ask for the same movement in the other direction. This system doesn't give as much opportunity to see the signals as in Join Up; you should still observe the licking and chewing as the horse comes in to you, but only to take note of what might be going on in your horse's mind. If you repeat this manoeuvre three or four times in either direction, inviting the horse in to you at the end of each occasion and praising him lavishly, you will soon find that when you unclip your horse he will stay close to you and follow after you, as he will prefer this option to moving around you.

Ideally, the line should only be there to stop him going too far away in a large area, maybe gently directing him but certainly not pulling him around at an unnatural angle.

**HAVING FUN WITH JOIN UP PIE CAN JUMP HIGHER THAN THIS, BUT UNFORTUNATELY HIS OWNER CAN'T.**

## MY CONCERNS ABOUT CONVENTIONAL LUNGING

Having a heavy cavesson on the horse's head and then attaching a line on the front of the nose puts an unnatural weight at this point and causes the horse to tip his head to the outside of the circle so that he counterbalances that weight. Horses are not designed to repetitively execute small circles, and it can damage joints, tendons and ligaments. Texas A & M University did a study in which researchers took x-rays of horses' legs before and after six weeks of light work on the lunge. This will often cause a horse to go disunited behind as well as putting stress on the back and legs. The results showed considerable unnatural calcification of the joints.

I have heard lunging recommended as a training method because it builds up muscle and is a way of teaching voice commands. With regard to building up muscle, I feel horses would be better off if people did long-lining with two reins to gain added control, and then applied a bilateral pressure so the horse can travel with his head directly in front of him or with the appropriate tilt, keeping the muscular, nervous and skeletal system in balance. Coupled with this, with two reins there is the potential for a far more stimulating time. Introduce some poles on the ground and changes of direction and transitions to keep up the interest. Once you are sure you are in control, consider going off round fields and tracks. This is a great way to exercise your horse and really encourages forward movement, an independent attitude and interest.

The problem with remedial horses that have been lunged excessively by well-meaning owners before they come to me, is they have been trained to 'switch off' to non-verbal communication from the handler. This is particularly the case if they never get asked in to the centre of the circle to stop the work, but are made to wait on the outside. Remember, a horse's natural way to asset leadership in the herd is to push another horse away from him. Yes, we can effectively incorporate their own use of discipline into our training of horses, but if you are effectively pushing that horse away for 20 minutes or more, you've got to consider how it might make that horse feel.

When I am dealing with any 'horse with problems' I want that horse to choose to come to me and stay with me, feeling that I am the safety zone. The constantly lunged horse will initially keep his gaze fixed to the outside of the ring and later in the walk will deliberately try to blank out any eye contact or body postures the handler makes. This can be overcome with a little prompting and lots of reward, but it seems a shame that the horse has been made to switch off from his natural form of communication in this way. Long-lining on two reins doesn't seem to have this effect; horses seem to know the difference between 'This is exercise mode now' and 'This is communication time'.

We do exercises from the ground or on the saddle that indicate pressure on one side means 'move over'; yet with lunging we put pressure on one side of the horse but demand him to go forward. Oregon trainer Chera Chase believes this is why trainers who lunge their horses regularly need the use of whips and spurs for lateral work. Why wouldn't the horse respond to your leg alone? Does he try to push forward instead? Perhaps he's misunderstanding your messages if his ground training is telling him pressure from the side means to move forward?

Lunging is the most popular exercise for remedial horses, and while it is a relatively safe option, I find it curious that people don't work more innovatively. You have got to think through clearly what it is exactly you are trying to achieve. It is most unlikely the horse is suddenly metaphorically going to throw his arms up and say, 'OK, OK, I've gone round in 300 circles now; I've got the point and I promise never to bolt, rear or nap again.' It could be one of those cases where because lunging is very easy and so is something the handler knows how to do, people do it for that reason alone. They may know in their heart of hearts it's not having any real benefit for the horse but they feel at least they are doing something. I hope after reading this book you will at least feel you have more options.

## SO YOU STILL WANT TO LUNGE?

If you've examined all the facts, considered there might be a better way for what you want to achieve but you still want to single-line lunge (it's quite undeniable that doing exercises off a lunged horse can be extremely beneficial to the rider), my suggestions would be:

• Find somewhere to attach the long line other than at the point of the nose, for example the back of the headcollar.

• Consider attaching correctly fitting elasticated side reins (obviously on a well-mouthed correctly schooled horse).

• Work in an enclosed area for safety and so as not to tempt the horse into pulling out of the circle.

• Encourage the horse to work in a large circle.

• Be sure the horse is working in the way you would want if he was being ridden, i.e. the hindlegs tracking the fore legs; make sure he's not learning bad habits.

• Always work on a good surface so as not to stress limbs unduly and be certain to keep the length of the sessions appropriate to the health and fitness of the horse.

• Read *Fit to Ride* by Mary Bromiley.

## WHEN TO USE JOIN UP
### 'ARE THERE ANY HORSES YOU SHOULDN'T DO JOIN UP WITH?'
First of all, I am assuming you have a quiet, well-handled horse of, say, two years old or more who is fully halter trained. Try to take him through the Foundation Exercises (see pages 58-73) first. However, do bear the following points in mind:

• With a very young horse or a horse that is very nervous, an inexperienced person sending him away could confuse him and do him more harm than good. Although you can go through the Join Up process with weanlings and foals, you need to work in a different way, similar to working with horses that can't be caught. You are trying to build their confidence up and want them to realize how nice it is to be with you. Sometimes they'll be trotting round the pen and think, 'I know I'll go into her – that'll please her!' If you raise your arms or slap the line on you, they'll think, 'Oops' she doesn't want me near her at all – I'd better stay out here!' When a horse is very young or nervous, you want to encourage every movement he makes to (respectfully) come closer to you. When he is older and more self-assured he'll understand that going away and turning are all part of the process and nothing to worry about.

If you want to go through the process with your youngster, do so only once, maybe twice. If you do more that that you may even find they get too 'Joined Up' and won't want to move away from you at all.

• Do not attempt Join Up with a horse that is in any way aggressive, because if you are inexperienced you can make matters worse. These horses are usually better off working on a training halter until they have figured out boundaries and learned to respect your space. If you are not used to working with colts and stallions, get to know them and become experienced with Join Up for some time before you consider putting the two together.

• Bottled-reared foals and even just over-handled foals very often don't learn their language while growing up and can become quite 'mixed-up kids', not popular with others of their species and having no respect for human beings and their space. If you are responsible for bringing up a foal, make sure you bring it up as a horse not as a baby. No matter how cute it seems, never have them cuddled on your knee or let them play games where they chase you. It's just asking for trouble. Foals need other youngsters to play with and again at weaning time require friends of their own age and size to play with and at the very least proper horse company. There isn't a great deal of value of Join Up for these types as their tendendy is to want to be too close to you anyway. There is more value working on the Foundation Exercises.

### 'HOW MANY TIMES SHOULD YOU USE JOIN UP?'

You use Join Up to create a bond with your horse, and once that's established it's unnecessary to keep going over the same process again and again. Using the technique three or four times when starting a young horse is fine; and if the horse has been off work for a while, or there is any sort of problem, you could go through the process once more to re-establish the relationship. A formal Join Up isn't something you need to do very often, but remember to use the same body language every day when handling your horse – be assertive when you need him to move back out of your space and passive when you go to catch him or when you want him to feel comfortable with you. If you go into an enclosed area with your horse loose and he chooses to stay with you then he's Joined Up quite enough already.

### 'MY HORSE ALREADY FOLLOWS ME EVERYWHERE. DOES THAT MEAN HE'S JOINED UP?'

Possibly, but not necessarily. If it's because he sees you as a fair and consistent leader and wants to be with you as his safety zone, or because the experiences you've shared have shown you to be trustworthy – well, yes, I suppose you can effectively say he's Joined Up. If he's just with you because you feed him titbits (a real no-no), or because he likes to push you around the school, or because he is nosey, then I'm afraid that isn't the same thing at all. It was Monty Roberts that actually coined the phrase Join Up, and it's his definition that the horse needs to go through the complete process before you can use the term.

## 'IS IT UNKIND TO SEND A HORSE AWAY?'

Sending a fit and mature horse around the pen is no more unreasonable than asking a horse to lunge or long-line, or trot a circle under saddle. Obviously, if you consider these things to be unfair to horses, which of course is your perfect right to do so, then you may also not like the idea of sending the horse around the pen. However, most of us, humans and horses alike, have to contribute something in life, and also learn to interact with each other as happily as possible. It's extremely important to bear in mind that, whatever role we have in life, we should never let a position of power allow us to turn into bullies or be insensitive to the feelings and needs of others. As I have already stated, if you are not getting a response within six minutes, the most likely reason is there is something you are misunderstanding, so you need to get expert help.

## 'WHEN CHANGING DIRECTION, SHOULD YOUR HORSE TURN AWAY FROM YOU OR TOWARDS YOU?'

With most horses I can usually control whether they turn towards or away from me by how I position my body, using eye contact and judging the speed of the horse. Using this mostly with older, more confident horses, I maintain strong eye contact, and 'square up' to them to turn them away from me. Pushing away like that is asserting my authority; if you didn't do it with a stallion, he may see it as a sign of 'weakness' and turn in to you and challenge you (not necessarily with unpleasant intent but with a 'Hey I'm ready to come in now so it's time!'). Another advantage of being able to turn the horse away is that when I eventually come to long-line the horse in the round pen, I need him to turn away otherwise the long lines get swirled around his legs like candyfloss on a stick.

With a very nervous horse, a youngster and perhaps a horse that is difficult to catch, I allow or even encourage him to turn in to me. I know this horse isn't intending to challenge me and I want to encourage any indication whatsoever he wants to come towards me or even just face me. Western trainers talk about horses having to get used to 'changing eyes'. Both sides of the horse's visual field need to be accustomed to different sights, and you need to work the horse from both directions. Even in the round pen, when a horse suddenly sees you out of a different eye, he can react as if the whole experience is new to him.

*teaching*

# GOOD

# MANNERS

# *first, catch* YOUR HORSE

Just as Mrs Beeton's famous household management book starts with the suggestion that you 'first catch your hare' before deliberating on which temperature to cook it at, so it is wise to be sure you can catch your horse before deciding how to cause him to produce the perfect pass/gallop/water jump or whatever accords with your present aspirations. This chapter looks at ways to do and ways not to do it. But first read about how the problem can start.

## HOW A PROBLEM CAN START

A problem with a horse can occur for many reasons:
- The handler's body language is appalling. She uses aggressive body language and movements.
- The horse is wild and unhandled.
- The horse is nervous or frightened of people in general or specifically his handler.
- The horse is turned out with a herd of other horses who don't want to be caught for any of the other reasons mentioned.
- The lead mare is leading the other horses off somewhere else. Also, in the case of foals, the mare's willingness to be caught will make a tremendous difference to the foal's attitude.
- The horse much prefers being out in the field with his friends and you only ever catch him when you want him to do some form of work. (He may have a point here.)

Catching a horse can be looked at in two distinctly different ways. One is to get close enough to him to get a rope round his neck so that you have him caught. The other is to get the horse to want to come to you and so be caught. Most people agree that the best state of affairs is to have the horse wanting to come to you. You want your horse to think: 'Hurrah! It's Daphne/Bertha/Bill/Insert Own Name.' So the question is: 'How do you make the horse want to do that?' Patience: all is to be revealed.

CLOSE ENCOUNTERS YOU NEED TO BE ABLE TO CATCH YOUR HORSE BEFORE MAKING TOO MANY OTHER PLANS FOR THE DAY.

## HOW NOT TO CATCH YOUR HORSE

Let's just recap here. If you want to send a horse away, you look him in the eye, walk at him squarely positioned and in a direct line, use excitable, jerky movements and act like a predator. When you get close enough, you go to 'grab' the horse, or if he isn't wearing a headcollar (make sure it's a breakable one if he's being turned out in it) you start waving the headcollar around and standing in front of him, trying to put his nose into it as quickly as possible.

## THINGS YOU CAN DO TO HELP

1 If you want to encourage a horse to come close, you keep your eyes 'soft' and looking down, you don't walk directly at the horse but walk as if you mean to go past him to start with, and you don't let your body face the horse but keep at an angle. If he has a headcollar on, after gently stroking him, maybe on his neck or somewhere he feels comfortable, you take the rope and using smooth motions, clip it directly to the back of the headcollar. If he's not wearing a headcollar, after the initial stroking you can stand alongside him to put it on. For a really nervous horse have the nose band undone, so you can put it on over his neck first and then do it up over his nose.

2 In the summer of 2000 we were sent at least five horses that came because they were 'impossible to catch'. These are good horses for us to be sent in the summer when we're running courses because they are very good 'teachers' for the students. Two of these horses were even difficult to catch in the stable. It doesn't take much intelligence to work out that they've got to be completely comfortable to be caught in the stable before you can even think of turning them out and expect them to be caught easily.

Basic polite manners of always presenting your head to people entering the stable should be the natural response from your horse. He should anticipate your arrival with pleasure and look forward to the nice stroke he'll receive from you. All horses need to learn to accept the halter helpfully in the stable, lowering their head to accept it. If this is not the case, and you have, in fact, 'a remedial horse' (see Turning his Bottom Towards You on page 120),

---

### THE WILD, UNHANDLED HORSE

It should go without saying that the horse we are talking about should have completed the Foundation Exercises (see pages 58-73), most importantly the one for being touched all over. He should also be really happy with his relationship with humans and be totally confident that they are not going to hurt him. If the lead mare is not wild and you can catch her, the other horses will generally all follow her so you can get them in a smaller catching area that way or alternatively get several people to help you 'herd' them into a smaller area. If you make this area a place where you provide the horse with food and water as well, he will soon look forward to coming in there.

you need to (literally) reverse this situation. A good method, using the horse's own language, as it were, is to 'square up' when he is turned away from you and be very positive the moment he turns to face you. Take on a rather 'Jekyll and Hyde' personality, but in a consistent way. With the nervous horse, ensure you are very gentle and give lots of reassuring strokes.

You then need to go over the Foundation Exercises, particularly 'touching all over' and leading the horse in circles round the box. Giving him a lovely rub as you finish each circuit will help him realize that he's meant to keep his head towards you. Only when you are sure your horse is absolutely comfortable with you in these circumstances do you want to take the next step of working in a round pen or larger enclosed area.

3 You can now take your horse into a round pen for a Join Up. Rather than 'send away' with any gusto, I suggest, to start with, you just make out that you are going out to catch him like someone using poor body language. Look him in the eye, walk directly towards him from a 45-degree angle behind, and use quite jerky motions and see what his

attitude is – remember this is your opportunity to learn more about your horse at the same time. Could there be genuine fear in his attitude? If the horse is showing any signs of fear, nervousness or concern, you need to take into account what was mentioned in the Join Up chapter (see previous chapter) with regard to nervous or young horses. In this case use very gentle body language, and if the horse makes any attempt to look at you at all, 'go submissive', dropping your eye contact and moving away from the horse. In other words, encourage each and every sign that shows he wants to be with you.

So we will let the horse tell us what is the best way to go in the round pen. If he is a cheeky, self-assured young man who is absolutely confident being handled once he is caught, we may work him quite hard with even a few circuits of cantering in the round pen in both directions before inviting him in. If we realize he clearly lacks confidence then we may decide just to gently walk after him in the round pen, actually 'mirroring' his movements.

**HOW CATCHING SHOULD BE THESE HORSES ALL WANT TO BE CAUGHT.**

*Case study*

# HOW TO CATCH 50 HORSES WITH A HOOTER

*When Monty Roberts was guest-lecturing on one of our courses, he told us all about his recent visit to a ranch where the owner ran about 50 head of riding horses out in the wild. They were hardworking horses used for gathering the 3000 or so cattle he owned. Monty wanted to see a foal from a particular stallion he was interested in, so the owner said, 'No problem, I'll just get them into the pens.' He drove to the top of a hill and started beeping his horn. The horses came cantering into the pen from up to three miles away! They were all given hay while they were in there, and Monty was told that was the routine every time they go in there. They are often called to the pens just to eat and then be turned out again.*

*There are three points the cattleman's story illustrates. Firstly, it's important to bring your horse in occasionally not to work – just to have a feed, a stroke and then go out again. Secondly, the cattle owner is making use of the herd mentality and the fact that horses are creatures of habit. He told Monty he would never just take a couple of the horses in and leave the others out, because once you start splitting them up and changing their habits you open a window for them to think negatively. As it stands, it is an enjoyable ritual for them and he has no horses that are hard to catch. The third important point is that his weanlings are turned out with the herd over a year before they are saddled, so that they also learn the system along with all the others.*

Mirroring means if he slows down in the slightest I slow down correspondingly; if he stops, I stop and go submissive. I will wait for a few moments and then make a gentle move towards him or to stroke him. If he moves off I'll just continue my very steady, persistent 'tracking' of him. If he goes faster, I walk after him, matching his pace. Once I've 'caught' these horses I tell them how wonderful they are, give the lovely rub and put them in the stable for a while with a nice, small feed.

With these horses, my eventual aim is to actually get them overly Joined Up. I will take them out in the round pen perhaps as much as three times a day and go through the same procedure. Very soon, maybe in just one day, the horse won't choose to go away from me at all; he'll very much prefer to follow me round the pen – which is exactly what I want. When the time comes that you can walk quite fast round the pen, changing direction, and he is still choosing to stay with you, then is the moment you can consider turning him out.

In an ideal world, the field should be no more than an acre or so, with not much to eat in it. It would be empty of other animals to start with, and in the later stages all the horse's companions would be really easy to catch; oh, and we'd have a small catching area by the gate, in case of any problems. Of course, it's not all that often we can have an ideal world but it's good to have one to aspire to.

4 The way you let him go is important, too. Leave him with a (breakable) headcollar on in these early stages, and as with any horse when you let him go, always have his head positioned towards you and the gate before releasing him. The point is, this 'releasing' needs to be as low key as possible in these circumstances. There may even be a case of taking some feed out in a bowl or bucket with you and let him have a little while he's just standing with you at the gate. What we need to do is 'blur the lines' in his mind as to when he is actually 'caught' or 'not caught'. Spend some time stroking him and let him just mosey off in a gentle manner.

Another idea is to let him go out initially while you're still holding a long line (mine are usually about 9m [30ft] long). Let him go out a little way, then bring him back in and pet him; let him go out again and then bring him back again and pet him. We want him to still feel psychologically attached to that line even when we take it off. This is how circus trainers work to obtain 'virtual lunging', i.e. their horses will react as if they are still on the line because they've done so much work on the line they've been 'brainwashed' and never think of testing if there have been any changes. Similarly, baby elephants are tied up when they are young, so they can be tied when they are older and not realize they could easily pull away. It's why I still do what my big sister tells me even though I'm bigger than her now.

### HORSES WITH PROBLEMS

The summer of 2000 was very satisfying from many points of view including our 'impossible to catch' cases, all of them improving very quickly indeed, three of them within a couple of days and the other two (who were 'fear' cases) within a week or so. Of course, we had to teach their owners to use the correct body language as well. One lady owner popped in unexpectedly with her children while we were admiring her pony that was turned out in the field. One of my students on the course gave her a quick lesson in body language (there is nothing like teaching to get you to learn a subject) and she went in with the pony, who then just followed her round faithfully. He'd only been with us two days and the owner couldn't believe it. Then each of her children went in with him and he did the same thing. They all said, 'This can't be the same pony, it just can't be the same pony!' (Incidentally, I do promise it was the same pony!)

5 You know those people who only ring you when they want something? You know how your heart sinks when you hear them on the phone? That's how your horse feels if you only ever go out to see him if it's for something for you. You need to take some time in going out to catch your horse just to give him a stroke, and then let him go away again (and make sure you ring your friends with good news for them occasionally as well).

Remember your body language. Just walk round in arcs in front of him with eyes down to start with, gradually getting closer, before going to take hold of him. He should have learned by now that if he turns round and faces you there is less chance of you 'irritating him' by throwing a line and pushing him away. When you get really proficient at body language/eye contact you will know how to make use of a quick glimpse into his eyes just to 'tease' him that you might push him away. This will bring him to attention very quickly if all the other training has been done thoroughly. Also, the best part is that the horse is so much happier with this deal because, of course, we are talking in a language he understands.

If you are carrying a headcollar, keep it over your shoulder for a while. Let him sniff the back of your hand first. When you get close, spend some time petting him, probably just his wither and shoulder to start with. Don't be tempted to grab his head. Gradually work your way up to his face and spend plenty of time stroking him before you bring out the halter. Sometimes you should catch him, bring him in for a feed and then turn him out again. If using food, when you get hold of him give him a lovely rub then just go away and leave him alone.

I suggest when you go to catch your horse for riding you always bring him in for a small feed first. If you get him to come in for a feed every day, whether you are riding him or not, that would be ideal. The horses at Willow Farm, where I run some of the courses, live in big herds and are called in to the barns for their feeds and a checkover every now and then. It is most impressive when Johnny Smith, the farm manager, makes a noise something like Tarzan's jungle cry and 40 black horses all come galloping towards the barns!

> Let a nervous horse first just sniff the back of your hand.

## FOOD, GLORIOUS FOOD

A way to make friends with a wary horse is to sit next to a bucket of food in a small paddock and let the horse make his own decision as to when to come up to the food and get close to you. You can eventually move on to gently stroking the horse and getting to know him. Try to ignore the horse completely at first so there is less pressure on him, and preferably read a book, (possibly this one, even) or depending on just how wary the horse is and your individual taste something like War and Peace or the Complete Works of Shakespeare may be more suitable.

The 'not over-feeding method' has been one of the secrets of the whisperers who can 'cure' a horse or pony of 'catching' problems and soon have him running up to see them. However, if all the components of the problem haven't been looked at, it would not only be very unfair to deprive a horse of food (and in some cases water), but there would also be a problem again as soon as he was given normal rations again.

The trouble with using food to catch horses if they are in a group is the danger of taking a bucket out and having them all crowding around you to get at the food. They can often start fighting with each other and a person can easily get hurt in the process.

Make a point of finding out what your horse's absolutely favourite food is. Carrots? Apples? One of the Pasture Mixes containing molasses?

After all, there are many of us who might not do something for beef burgers, whereas we may be swayed by chocolates and champagne. Whichever method you decide to use (and it's best to have as many tricks up your sleeve as possible), just be sure you are working with the psychology and nature of the horse and not just looking at things from a human viewpoint: 'He is deliberately doing this because he knows I can't be late for work today!' Soon you'll have a horse that positively wants to be 'caught'.

### A NOTE ABOUT CATCHING PONIES

We talk about using body language and eye contact for communication with horses, but this is not so useful if we are way above the pony and the only area level to their eyes is the top of our legs. You sometimes hear of ponies that children can catch but not adults. Most horses and ponies dislike anything unfamiliar that is towering above their heads. The simple solution here is that, for some ponies, you need to crouch right down when approaching them or use submissive body positioning.

## PLANS FOR THOSE EMERGENCY SITUATIONS

For the horse that can be caught with a treat but tends to snatch it then run off, one method is to have a piece of string hanging about 15 cm (6 in) from the back of his (breakable) headcollar. You approach the horse holding both your hands together with the empty hand slightly in front of the hand holding the tasty treat. Most horses once they know they are 'caught' quickly acquiesce. If this is not the case and he's likely to pull away, much more leading training work is needed.

### JUST PULLING HIS LEG

I've heard it working for some older horses that you don't go to their head but you bend down to look at their leg. This can catch a horse totally by surprise as you bend down and ask him to pick up his leg and hold up the leg on the nearside with your right hand while taking his headcollar or slipping a rope over his neck with your left hand. A horse must feel a bit of a fool when he's been caught this way.

### ARE YOU GOING BACKWARDS?

Well, you could try it. Again, this 'odd' behaviour can sometimes take a horse by surprise enough for you to get the job done. It's curious to watch when this does work. The horse just watches in amazement.

### FOR WHEN YOU'RE AT THE END OF YOUR TETHER

Yes, tethering is an option if things have really got that bad. Certainly people going on excursions will tether the horses at the camp side. Personally, I wouldn't feel happy tethering a horse that wasn't within view.

# *perfect manners*
# AT HOME

## HORSES THAT BARGE AND TREAD ON YOU
## (OR, 'GET OUT OF MY SPACE!')

### HOW THIS PROBLEM STARTS

A horse that walks all over you is most definitely very rude. However, responding with unsophisticated yelling and bashing is not going to do you any credit or, indeed, help the situation. Let us consider the possible causes:

• The horse has never been taught any differently.

• The horse is distracted by other horses (see also Neighing and Making a Fuss, pages 140-2).

• The horse is much bigger than the handler, has his head up high and can't see her.

• The handler has low self-esteem and invites all and sundry to take advantage of her.

### THINGS YOU CAN DO TO HELP

1 The horse needs to be taught that he must respect your personal space and this will easily be solved once you have completed the Foundation Exercises successfully (see pages 58-73). However, if you are having problems even as you are doing the Foundation Exercises, it may be that you need to consider two of the above points very seriously. Do some people invite others to tread all over them? I think we all know the answer – I'm afraid so. Do all small people get trodden on? Absolutely not. What's going on here? Well, it's all down to 'intention'. We tend to get what we believe and what we expect. So if we've always been trodden on, and don't realize we have a right to expect anything different, it's going to keep right on happening.

2 We need to believe that we have a right to be treated well and to have others respect us (including our horses). This doesn't mean we need to be aggressive – just assertive. We need to know our boundaries

**STANDING STILL TO MOUNT**
IT'S SO MUCH MORE
CONVENIENT IF YOUR HORSE
WILL STAND STILL FOR YOU.

put it: 'Four of those horses killed themselves.' They died during the swinging process, as they were each tied to a wall and left to fight it out. Two of the horses were killed by crushing their heads, two died of a broken neck. Bad injuries can be caused as well, purely by accident, by someone tying an untrained horse to a fence and the horse breaking away, taking part of the fencing with him, which appears to 'chase him' as he runs in terror. Please take heed.

Most people in England tie their horses to a piece of orange string attached to a metal ring. (Orange string lurks in every nook and cranny of stable yards round Britain.) This is because, if the horse panics, the string will break rather than breaking the headcollar or hurting the horse. If a horse hasn't been properly taught to let himself be tied and gets in the habit of breaking the string, he gets to know if he just pulls hard enough he can break away. Every time he succeeds, he reinforces this behaviour, making him more confident in his strength for every future attempt, and this can become a very difficult habit to break.

'Cures' with elastic bungee ties can be very dangerous if every part of the process and equipment isn't examined thoroughly. If something breaks, it can act like a missile, and horse (and human) eyes are easily lost that way. With these risks I strongly advise a cost/risk analysis. How important is it to you that this horse will let himself be tied up? Is this method worth the potential risks? The point of these horror stories is to make you very aware of the possible dangers. Personally, I would always go back to the beginning and retrain a horse rather than trying to go for the quick fix – particularly in this case. Be sure to do sufficient preparatory work before you even think about tying your horse. He must know how to release himself from any pressure before going for the first lesson in being tied up.

### THINGS YOU CAN DO TO HELP

We need to teach our horses the 'Three Rs' – Request, Response, Release – and to understand that when they feel pressure they need to let themselves go with it. We need to go over those Foundation and Yielding Exercises (see pages 58-85) until we reach perfection. Any 'sticking points' need to be worked at again in order to 'oil the wheels' – as you keep working, the horse becomes more and more malleable. Making your horse sensitive to pressure in the right way will have many other advantages: for instance, if your horse accidentally steps on his reins, instead of the usual panic and broken reins, he will understand to just nod his head down until he thinks out how to release himself.

Carry out various yielding tests to ensure the horse completely understands. Another interesting 'test' I haven't mentioned earlier is to stand with your horse and put the rope from his headcollar over his head and pull gently down. If your horse throws his head and resists, he's not ready to be tied yet. Work with him so that he understands again to yield to that pressure and that bringing his head down will take the pressure away.

1 For the first lesson in tying, I find it is best to have a metal ring placed high, about level with the horse's ears, and then I place a long rope, about 3.6m (12ft) long, on to the horse's headcollar, through the metal ring and back into my hand. I don't try and pull the horse tight to the ring but I move around him in a workmanlike manner on both sides and if he backs up at all I just gently ask him to step forward with a 'giving' pressure on the rope. It's when the rope is pulled solidly, as if from a fixed source, that it causes the horse to rear and resist. The ring is placed high so that as the horse's head is held up his back goes down, and this doesn't put him in a strong position to pull.

2 Before actually tying, it's essential to test the horse's reactions when there are a few distractions around – another horse walking by, for instance. Then have someone walk behind with a noisy bucket or simulate any of the usual (or unusual) distractions that can be around. Once he understands this simple concept, 'To stop the pressure just take a step towards where it's coming from', your horse is ready to be tied. Go through this routine once more when asking him to let himself be tied on to the side of a horsebox or a fence, just to be on the safe side. You can test your horse's reactions further by gently shaking some plastic bags round him or being deliberately provocative. The trick here is to 'doubly reward him': shake the bag, or whatever, and then as soon as he goes forward to release the pressure, reward him by stopping the stimulus (i.e. the shaking) at the same time.

When first tying your horse, have a quick-release knot and a safety system in place. Also tying to something elasticated, such as a tyre's inner tube, is a good idea so that the horse won't meet a solid resistance if anything were to happen, and he is far less likely to panic.

We have never had a problem with tying up horses when bringing them on ourselves – it's a natural, easy, transition in their training. Having a horse stand tied comfortably outside, eating from his haynet and seeing everything going on, can be of great benefit to a horse and help build his confidence generally. As with all horse training, doing the preliminary training thoroughly and thoughtfully in the first place saves time and effort in the long run, as it avoids taking time-consuming measures to retrain your horse.

If you have an older horse who has learned to pull back and consistently does so, there are forms of 'ground tying' that may work with your horse. Just draping a long line over a fence and repeatedly moving your horse back if he moves away can work very well. If the horse never gets his 'fix' of feeling the rope snap and breaking away, he may, over a period of several months, forget all about the habit.

## GROUND TYING

What a luxury to have a horse that you can leave anywhere in the countryside and he will stand and wait for you. How sophisticated can you get! I wouldn't recommend ground tying for every horse. If you have an extremely valuable competition horse, you are no more likely to drop the reins and leave him to stand alone as you are to put your Rolex watch on a shelf while you do your shopping at a supermarket. However, for the horse whose worth doesn't lie in those rather obvious attributes, an 'optional extra' like this can produce just as much envy.

## THINGS YOU CAN DO TO HELP

First your horse must have been taught to yield and be tied normally, to an advanced standard, and then there are two ways to achieve similar results, depending on what you feel is the most practical. What I sometimes use is some light thin cord that can easily be carried in my pocket when I'm riding. After doing all the other Foundation and Yielding exercises on the thicker lead, I start to see if he can now start to follow the thinner lead. (Note: I do not take the thinner lead round his body, and I always wear gloves for this. Never wrap any rope round your bare hands or fingers when working with horses.)

1 Once I am confident my horse can follow even this tiny signal, I start to test tying him to just a piece of hedge. As with all our training we test this out in smaller areas first, then a larger field; and soon it has some really practical applications when out in the countryside, particularly if you ever had to leave your horse alone for a few minutes in an emergency.

2 Another method is to drop a normal, heavier-weight rope on the floor in front of your horse as the cue for him to stand and wait until you go back to him. You have already worked along these lines with the 'standing' and 'handling all over' Foundation Exercises.

3 You can move up to a more advanced level with the handling all over by introducing your horse to more disturbing objects. Three of my students once did a horse psychology project, based on one used by the German army who were desensitizing mules to prepare them to go into the front line. Everything from plastic bags, umbrellas, toys and loud noises were used. It even got to the stage where they could run at the horse waving and shouting and the two-year-old filly, Delia, would just stand there, totally ignoring them, completely undisturbed. She became quite literally 'bomb proof' and you could have let your great-

granny hold her with no worries. It shouldn't have been a surprise, therefore, when we came to do Join Up (see pages 86-107) with this youngster a few months later that there was no way the handler could send her away from them! Do be sure when you are training your horse that you are clear as to when he is meant to react and when he is not meant to react.

Again, for this exercise your horse needs to have learned to yield to the minimal of pressure. This is because you want him to respect the pressure of the rope on the floor, and also because if he were to tread accidentally on the rope (which can happen), we'd want him to yield and put his head down, rather than panic and throw his head up.

4 Voice requests are very helpful for teaching ground tying as well. (See The Use of the Voice in Training, pages 49-54). You can start by asking your horse to 'stand', and dropping your 3.6m (12ft) lead rope down in front of him, keep facing him but take a few steps backwards. If he moves at all, immediately go back and put him back in position. After he has stood for, say, 30 seconds, go back to him and tell him how good he is. Gradually progress with this exercise until you can stand further and further away and he will stand still for longer periods of time. After each period go back and stroke him. You may have guessed: this exercise is much easier to do on an area without grass.

**THE VALUE OF GROUND TYING** HAVING A HORSE THAT CAN BE GROUND TIED IS QUITE A LUXURY. PIE IS EXTREMELY VALUABLE, BUT ONLY TO ME.

Eventually, you want to be sure he'll stand even when you walk away with your back turned towards him. Once you are sure your horse is 100 per cent trustworthy, it's for you to decide the practical applications of this. I've known of racehorse trainers' 'hacks', riding instructors' and huntsmen's horses that will stop and wait patiently while the rider deals with any emergency. A horse that will do this can be worth his weight in gold.

## BITING
### HOW THIS PROBLEM STARTS

• Engaging in forms of play with the horse, particularly stallions or colts. It's something that colts are very likely to 'experiment with' at some stage in their upbringing.

• Not ensuring your horse has regular checks from an equine dental technician.

• Allowing the horse's teeth to become sharp, which could make him feel the need to bite things to relieve the pain. Young horses losing their baby teeth, or having trouble with their 'caps', will often become very nippy.

• Doing things that hurt the horse or make him uncomfortable, for example putting on a badly fitting saddle, doing the girths up roughly, throwing rugs on badly, putting a bridle on clumsily. There are so many instances where people are inconsiderate to their horses and handle them roughly.

> ### 'LISTEN TO WHAT I'M TRYING TO SAY'
> A horse who has been trying to communicate by more subtle means – moving away to the back of the stable as the saddle is brought in, or making anxious faces, for example – may have to resort to biting to make people notice his predicament.

• Rough grooming is a particularly common example. It can be quite painful for a horse to have mud removed from a sensitive area.

• Irritating the horse – bothering him when he is eating, speaking incessantly in a high-pitched voice, fiddling around endlessly with potions and creams and a hundred different rugs. Some horses love this attention, others prefer the least amount of fuss. The opposite of this is not giving the horse enough attention – some horses are like some children, and would rather have negative attention than no attention. If you think this may be the case, make a point of increasing the time you're with your horse, fussing and stroking him in the way he likes. Just make sure you don't do this in immediate response to an unacceptable demand from him – he shouldn't be pushing you around or forcing you to give him a head rub.

• Depriving the horse of social interaction with other horses, so that he feels the need to engage in his natural 'horsing around' behaviour with humans. This is often the case with stallions and colts, who naturally use their teeth a lot when interacting with other horses, and who tend to be isolated throughout their lives.

• Depriving the horse of any freedom – many horses don't adapt well to living inside permanently, and it can cause them to become stressed.

• If a horse has ever been starved or kept short of food so that he has felt seriously deprived, he can be touchy around his food.

• Engaging in mutual grooming – some horses work out that they need to be very gentle, and only use their top lips; others use their teeth. If you do want to be friendly with your horse in this way, set suitable boundaries, make sure you initiate the session, and don't allow it to lead to full-scale biting. Never do it with a horse who already has a tendency to bite; it will only confuse him.

• Feeding the horse titbits and allowing him to become very pushy with his nose. Eventually he may take pockets off with his teeth in his search for treats. Some horses never become rude and are very gentle when fed from the hand, but for so many it seems to blur the boundaries and lead to pushiness and a lack of respect. With this type of horse, it is very important never to feed them by hand, and never allow them to frisk you for treats.

• Playing with the horse's mouth. This also gives the horse the idea that it's all right to put his mouth on you. Again, with some horses this can be absolutely safe; with others it's a good way to lose a finger. Know your horse, and act accordingly.

• Any horse who has been beaten up may well develop aggression and biting as a defence mechanism, as you could well understand.

One of the major requests for 'quick-fix solutions' I receive is for biters. There seem to be an extraordinary amount of horse owners getting bitten every day. It's even more extraordinary that having worked with horses all my life and knowing many people who work in racing yards, show yards and studs, you'll find it's actually pretty rare among experienced horsepeople. So what's going on? What is it that inexperienced horsepeople do differently? A combination of two things, I feel. Firstly, a horse is far more likely to bite someone timid and hesitant who lacks confidence. Some people seem to give out vibes of: 'I'm a lowly earthworm. Come here and bite me. Come over and tread on me.' I'm sorry if this offends anybody, but it's true! This is why if you want to cure your horse of biting, it's very important for the two of you to work together on the problem. It can be very difficult to 'cure' somebody else's horse of biting, because what happens so often is the horse won't even try to bite you but then when he goes back to his owner he starts again (see the 'Cheeky Arabian' on the next page).

Then, of course, there is the opposite end of the scale, where people operate purely from blind faith. It's all too easy to want to believe ridiculous statements of the kind I heard from one 'expert': 'If you don't

Let's try and make common sense common practice by thinking less of how to punish the horse after he's bitten us and more about how to avoid getting bitten in the first place.

think a horse will bite you, then he never will! That's crazy! I knew one horse that used to fly over his door at unsuspecting people when they had no idea he was even there. So, secondly, when experienced people are around a horse that might bite – i.e. maybe a hyped-up stallion, or a horse giving clear signals that he's not happy – they are extremely careful, respectful of the damage he may cause, and they don't take any silly risks.

If you have a horse that bites sometimes, I suggest that you ask yourself: 'Is there anything I could be doing that is making this horse want to bite me?' 'Is there anything from this horse's past that is making him want to bite people?' 'How can I make it far less likely that my horse wants to bite me?' 'How can I generally keep myself in positions and situations where I am unlikely to be bitten?'

## THINGS YOU CAN DO TO HELP

As with all problems, the first step is to find out why the horse is biting. This will put you on the right path. After addressing that issue, then completing the Foundation Exercises (see pages 58-73) is the next step to take. A horse that stands at a respectful distance away from you, and moves away in any direction you request, is less likely to try to take chunks out of you. Of course, in the process of teaching him these movements, a confirmed biter may respond with his teeth. So how should you respond to this situation?

I have had the marvellous Lucy Rees (author of the excellent book *The Horse's Mind*) in to give a guest lecture to my students on several occasions, primarily because I love to take any opportunity to study and appreciate all the different ideas that experienced and innovative horsepeople may have. On the first occasion that Lucy lectured, the subject came up of what she might do if a horse were to bite. 'I'll show you,' said Lucy and with that she seemingly went into a complete fit; screaming and shouting at the top of her voice and waving her

### SILLY MOTHER

I get many letters about problems with horses and this is a typical letter:

*'Please, please help me. My pony is lovely in every way, he wins lots of competitions and I love him very much. His only problem is he is very bad-tempered when there is food about. He has been fine for ages but the other day I was grooming him and my mum was feeding him carrots. He kept dropping some of the carrots and the third time my mum went to pick them up for him he bit her on the shoulder. The vet now says I should have him put down. Please help me and my pony.'*

A letter like this is so sad. It may well be that the pony is not suitable for a child at all. However, it's quite obvious that the mother is not experienced with ponies, and really, if she knows the pony is 'funny' about his food (he's probably been kept hungry at some stage – maybe other ponies have kept him away from his food), what on earth is she doing feeding him carrots and picking them up in front of him in the first place?

*Case study*

## CHEEKY ARABIAN

*I have never seen a clearer example of this than at a Monty Roberts' horse demonstration at Eaglesfield Equestrian Centre in Kent. Monty was asked to work with a very beautiful, two-year-old Arab colt whose owner had experienced trouble handling him, but particularly with biting. The colt came in and just refused to put one foot wrong. He stopped when Monty stopped, walked when Monty walked, and made the audience laugh a couple of times when he looked around at the audience with this expression on his face that said, 'Me? Do anything wrong? Never!' Monty worked with him for five to ten minutes to illustrate a couple of points but this young colt gave us all the impression that he wouldn't even know how to think a bad thought. The owner was surprised and a little embarrassed as she came to lead him out, but you could see as soon as she took him how his whole attitude changed to someone who was back in charge. Just as she was going through the door of the school, I saw him take his first little nip ...*

arms in the air. This carried on probably for only a minute but it seemed much longer, as the whole class, including myself, sat in complete shock. Lucy explained at the end of this demonstration, 'If you do something like that, a horse will rarely ever think about biting you again.' I can believe that!

1 Overreacting can be surprisingly effective – respond to a bite as if you've been stung by a wasp – jump around in an exaggerated fashion or really square up to your horse. If you are holding him on a long enough line you could square up and push him to the end of the line and send him around a few times, or in a round pen you can push him right away for a circuit or two. He can come back and stay with you on the condition that he's going to 'be nice'. A lot of horses will reform quickly to avoid eliciting this kind of reaction. You may want to explain to anyone who's watching that this is a deliberate ploy – you haven't suddenly turned into a maniac. (On the other hand, after one of these outbursts, you'll notice them move round you with a degree of awe and respect as well).

*❝ It is so easy to fall into that trap of dealing with the symptoms rather than the real causes. ❞*

*Case study*

# THE 'VISCIOUS' GELDING

*Last winter I was asked to deal with a 'viscious' horse and after seeing the scar on the owner's arm, believe me I was respectful of this young gelding. I worked with this youngster, establishing boundaries and respect, for long enough to get him ridden and various people who worked round him soon found, although taking no chances, he was easy for them to catch safely and quite good in the stable. I asked the owner to come up and see him because I felt he was a great deal safer now. I was showing the owner how I handled him and how good he was and encouraged her to come and 'give him a stroke'. She demurred at first but after assurances from me she finally came up to the horse. What she did next made my blood run cold. She put her face directly under his mouth, nose less than 8 cm (3 in) away, and with both hands proceeded in tickling his lips with all her fingers! Something clicked for me then about how some people are far more likely to receive nasty bites than others.*

If you need to go and look at a horse in, say, a field or a round pen and you seriously think he may attack you, an umbrella is a useful defence item. If the horse comes at you and you immediately open up the umbrella, it generally surprises him just long enough to keep him away from you while you decide on your next move – like getting out of there.

come and push you around or put their mouth on you.

Be warned that if a horse has ever been starved, or kept short of food so that he felt seriously deprived, he is going to be touchy around his food. I had a lady ring and tell me: 'My horse has always been really defensive about his food and then one night I started to change his rugs while he was having his evening feed and he bit me!' The answer has to be, 'Yes, I'm sure he did!' I think sometimes horse owners have in their minds what horses should or shouldn't do, without applying a great deal of common sense.

## YOUNGSTERS WHO BITE

It's very natural for youngsters, particularly colts, to nip or try to bite you, just as human babies can bite their mothers when they are teething or through a 'I wonder what would happen if I do this?' type of curiosity. Usually a flinch and a loud 'Ow!' is enough to discourage this. Certainly just squaring up to horses momentarily before going back to being perfectly normal, is more than enough, and keep a boundary around you and their mouths away from your skin.

However, to hurt or frighten a young horse at this stage in an effort to 'show him it's wrong' can seriously backfire, as in the case of the ex-racehorse I was talking about. A frightened, insecure horse can become most dangerous as he literally feels he has to protect his own life.

With these horses as well, you never, ever feed them titbits from your hands and never play around their lips with your fingers. This advice is also good for any youngster that you don't want to get into the bad habit of raiding your pockets, which will soon turn to nibbling you. Don't let foals start suckling on your fingers or nibbling at the buttons on your coat. It's unfair to encourage them along this path, because it's so 'sweet' to start with, and then later be angry with them when this behaviour has evolved into biting.

However patient your horse, avoid irritating him in any way when at all possible. Grooming (see pages 159-60) should be a pleasant experience and if everyone could study some of Mary Bromiley's massage techniques I am sure it could only improve horses' lives and temperaments. Nowadays, grooming often seems to have degenerated into a few quick, brisk strokes with a hard bristle brush to get the horse presentable for riding. A soft brush with long, slow strokes is more relaxing for the horse. If the horse is encouraged to stretch his neck out and receive a comforting massage, he will be far less likely to want to bite or nip in irritation.

Another time where I often see inconsiderate behaviour to the horse is when people put on horse saddles or rugs and drop them with a thump on to the horse's back and then throw the girths of surcingles over the top so the buckles smack against the horse's tendons. It should go without saying that the saddle, indeed all equipment, and the positioning of the rider should be comfortable for the horse so he doesn't look on the experience with distaste.

## UNFRIENDLY FACES
### HOW THIS PROBLEM STARTS
• Horses often learn this from other horses; one 'face maker' in the yard can start off a whole string of admirers all competing to be the meanest-looking horse in the yard.

• The handler can then ingrain this further by stepping around the horse very nervously. The horse soon discovers he has a useful tool; he starts to think, 'Hey – maybe I am a big, tough kid after all!' Once again, 'inadvertent training' has taken place.

---

### HORSES PROTECTIVE OF THEIR FOOD
The secure horse may enjoy a stroke down his neck as he's eating but it's best to organize yourself so that you can leave the insecure horse totally alone at this time. Sometimes it works best to put the feed in when your horse is out of his box, then lead him into the box, turn his head to the door, let him loose and leave him alone. Try as much as possible not to make food a highly charged issue by ensuring he has access, even if only for a short time if he's overweight, to forage at all times. So many horses are brought in at 5pm and given a small haynet and a hard feed. By 8pm there'll be no food left. This can mean something like 11 hours without food. Many horses may be better off with continuous feeds of hay, and no hard food, just a vitamin lick. Ideally, someone should look in on stabled horses late in the evening to check that they have enough hay and water to see them through the night. This over-protectiveness of food is most likely to arise with a horse that has been starved or a horse that was bottle-reared/overhandled/wrongly 'imprinted' as a foal. The latter type will tend to think of you more as a (rather weak) companion than the person in charge and won't back off easily. Round-pen work can improve all types of animal by encouraging them to respect and yield to you, but I still advise you to not court danger at feed times until you really feel you are in control.

---

**A GOOD ACTOR (OVERLEAF)**
WITH BODY LANGUAGE YOU CAN TRAIN A HORSE TO ACT NAUGHTY – MAKE SURE YOU'RE NOT DOING IT ACCIDENTALLY.

## THINGS YOU CAN DO TO HELP

1 With these non-serious types it's often just a question of calling their bluff, making sure you move around them confidently, ignoring the grumpy faces and giving plenty of strokes and rewards as soon as they are ready to be pleasant and polite. There is sometimes a case here for a little food in a bowl – definitely not as a bribe, but as a reward for when the 'nice face' is on – which may help the horse genuinely look forward to seeing you.

2 Sadly, though, there are some horses that use these faces as a genuine defence as they have suffered cruel or thoughtless treatment. Continuous kind treatment is going to have the best results, but study the section on 'Biting' above to ensure you are doing your best to not aggravate the situation further and to ensure you keep safe.

### A GOOD ACTOR

It is difficult if your horse has already been trained into biting people. When I say 'trained' I mean inadvertently trained; but fully trained nevertheless. I saw a wonderful *National Geographic* feature about a French horse trainer and stuntman by the name of Mario Luraschi. M. Luraschi had trained a horse to be 'savage' for the films. The feature shows the horse charging at him, stopping a few feet away and lashing out with his front feet and his teeth snapping dangerously close. He then turns around and kicks out a couple of times for good effect.

All the time M. Luraschi is waving a stick at him, desperately 'defending' himself. Then the horse is given a signal and he knows the game is over. He goes over to the trainer for a nice head rub and rest. 'He's the kindest horse you could have,' says Luraschi.

I show this feature to my students on the five-day course because I want them to be aware that you can literally train a perfectly nice horse to show all the signs of being vicious and that some people do this without realizing what's happening. The first time a horse makes an unpleasant face at his owner and they back off quickly, he thinks, 'Oh this is good!' and soon starts working on a repertoire.

### NEIGHING AND MAKING A FUSS

'Separation anxiety' is a term that originated in child psychology for a child or adolescent who goes through fear, depression or panic to an abnormal degree and for an abnormal length of time when he or she was separated from their home or parents. The label then started to be used for dogs that adopt frantic behaviour if they are ever left alone at home, and is one of the most common reasons owners seek professional advice for pet behaviour. Now one often hears this term used for horses as well. Such is progress! Here's an example of the effect of words: 'He's got separation anxiety' puts one into a far more positive mindset than, 'He's a ridiculously noisy lunatic as soon as the other horses leave him!'

### HOW THIS PROBLEM STARTS

• In the wild, being separated from the herd is one of the most terrifying things that can happen to a horse, making him feel isolated and vulnerable. It's completely normal for a stallion to be frustrated if any mares are taken away, but in fact, in the absence of stallions, many geldings will take on the 'protector role' and be very unhappy if a mare or mares are removed. Particularly in the field, the gelding runs up and down the fence, neighing and calling. Many horses form close same-sex bonds, which is quite natural, and two mares often bond strongly.

• It's also quite normal for mares and foals to be distressed if they are separated, and this occurs particularly at weaning time. It is the key time when many stereotypical 'vices' such as crib biting, wind sucking, weaving and box walking start. An all-too-common way of weaning is to shut the foal in a stable with the top door closed for several days while the mare is taken away. This must be the most traumatic method available.

## THINGS YOU CAN DO TO HELP

1 A secure domestic horse should be able to develop a certain amount of independence. If you find you have problems with a particular horse, correct management is often a major part of the solution. If you have a horse that seems particularly clingy, perhaps avoid pairing a mare predisposed to this problem to another mare, and similarly, with a gelding, try to pair it with another gelding. There's never any point in you getting upset with them; they can't help what they're feeling. All you'll be doing is adding another problem to the equation.

Some racehorses I've known seem to have permanent free-floating anxiety, possibly coming from being highly strung and being weaned unsympathetically. Having a sheep or goat permanently in their stable, and even travelling with them to keep them company, seems to make them feel more secure.

2 When weaning, it's ideal if there are several mares and foals out together, and at around six months one mare at a time can be taken away over a period of a week or so until the foals are all left with just each other for company.

3 Another method I have heard of working well is 'nutritionally' weaning at around six months, but allowing the mare and foal to still see each other. You can do this by putting them in separate fields on the opposite side of secure fencing so they can still see each other but the foal can't suckle. They should each have other companions on their own side for the fence for company. The mare is usually pleased with the well-earned rest from feeding the foal, but feels reassured that she can still see him. One of the prime causes of mastitis in mares is the stress that the initial separation from the foal causes them. After two to three weeks, when the mare's milk has dried up, the mare and foal

can be completely separated, if it is felt necessary at that time. Natural weaning takes over nine months to a year. There is no reason why a foal's early training and handling can't take place while he is still unweaned. Do consider all the options available to you.

4 One way to prevent horses from panicking if they are to be left alone is to regularly expose them to short separations from their companions. The key is to find other ways to distract them during this time, either with feed, or spending some time grooming them, or doing a few Foundation Exercises (see pages 58-73) with them to try and keep their attention and concentration. The length of time can be gradually increased. Remember, a youngster doesn't know if his friend has disappeared for ever or will be back shortly. Once he starts to have more confidence his friend or friends will return, he'll be able to relax.

I've never known of a horse getting upset about a human leaving in the same way as he would about another horse, although I have known horses show every sign of being happy to see a person arriving, and we can do our best to provide some of the companionship they need if appropriate horses aren't available. We must always bear in mind that the horse is a naturally gregarious, herd animal and company is very important to him.

### GOLDEN FIRE AND LUCY, HIS SHEEP

My father had a very good racehorse some years ago by the name of Golden Fire. (He was too important to have a shortened name.) Before he arrived Golden Fire had run in races but was described as 'useless', having once run completely off the course in a selling race. He was a type 'A' personality, easily stressed, who used to throw himself on the ground when he first came to the yard. My father thought getting him a stable companion might help – hence a sheep called Lucy became his live-in companion. When Golden Fire went on exercise, Lucy would look out at the end of the drive for him when he was due to come in. Golden Fire's whole personality changed, he became far more secure and less defensive and went on to be a very successful racehorse, winning the Chester Cup, the Goodwood Stakes (twice) and the Cesarewitch; and Lucy the sheep travelled everywhere with him. This was because, although Golden Fire appeared unconcerned, Lucy got very distressed if he was away for any length of time.

Appreciating this, and making use of this in different ways, can help our training as the case study above illustrates. The more time we spend with our horse and doing specific things together – the Foundation Exercises, Join Up, riding – will all help to build our relationship and give them other things to think about.

### SCRAPING DOORS AND FLOORS — EVERYTHING
#### HOW THIS PROBLEM STARTS
• Scraping is a sign of frustration. It is often a displacement activity.
• The horse is not getting enough food/attention/companionship.

*Case study*

# MAKING FRIENDS WITH A COLT

*A while ago I was asked to work and start a two-and-a-half-year-old colt, who had never been separated from his mother. He had never been trained to be led properly because they couldn't do anything if his mother wasn't with him and, even is she was, they still had difficulties catching him.*

*The first day I thought I'd try a Join Up (see pages 86-107) with the colt. He was so worried about being on his own he didn't even see me there in the round pen with him. I went out of the round pen and the colt was still running around and neighing, calling to other horses for help and reassurance, obviously not trusting me enough to stand still and let me catch him. In order to catch him and stop the stress (by now I was concerned), we needed to bring his mother in and then catch him, so I could do a little work to finish as much as I could in a positive way.*

*I was sure that in order to work with the colt I needed him to gain his trust in me, and then let me get close enough to put a halter on, but the million-dollar question was 'How?' First, I needed to catch him, but that wasn't going to happen, so the next day I put him in a small round pen and left him alone there with his water and a little hay. The colt was neighing and calling to other horses, but no horse came, only me with a halter. The colt still wouldn't let me go to him, so if that was his decision, I thought, 'That's OK' and just let him be alone in the round pen again. After 30 minutes I went to catch him again; this time he stopped neighing, stood still and looked at me. He wouldn't let me put the halter on him, so again I left him alone.*

*This procedure went on a few more times. After a while, every time the colt saw me come over, he'd stop looking for other horses and start looking at me for reassurance and confidence. He started to understand that it was only me that came to his help every time that he called, so at the end it was his decision to stand still and trust me and let me catch him.*

*I didn't fight or argue with his decision not to stand still. I let him live with the consequences of his decision. By the end of the day the colt would stand still and look forward to seeing me. With this complete change of attitude and trust, we were able to continue happily.*

**INTELLIGENT HORSEMANSHIP RECOMMENDED ASSOCIATE DAVID GRODEK**

•Inadvertent training. The horse is scraping because of frustration at wanting his food. If the handler immediately arrives with his food, the horse will believe that this is the way to get the food 'reward'.

• He's feeling frustration for other reasons, including waiting around or being uncomfortable.

• He sees other horses doing it and copies them.

• It may not be a problem that has been 'developed' particularly; it's just a behaviour that the horse performs every time he's frustrated.

• Horses have a natural inclination to scrape at their feed on the stable floor and will also sometimes scrape their feed mangers if they are on the floor.

THINGS YOU CAN DO TO HELP
In all these cases I would try to think out how to 'manage' the behaviour and cause him not to want to scrape, rather than 'cure' it altogether. After all, it is part of the horse's basic rights to state when he is frustrated!

1 With the horse that scrapes for food you may find that preparing each feed in advance, i.e. while he's eating the meal before, means that he doesn't have to go through the torture of listening to you prepare his feed while he's hungry. Horses are naturally trickle feeders so the more their eating can be spread out during the day, with lots of high-fibre, low-energy feed, the less stress is going to be involved with it. Consider a 'horse ball' for him to play with.

2 Try to avoid putting your horse in a situation where he is likely to experience frustration. After spending the time on the Foundation Exercises and helping him overcome any separation anxiety (see also Neighing and Making a Fuss, pages 140-2), really he should be able to stand quietly in various situations. However, if he's still young and inexperienced, it's a lot to expect for him to just stand there while, for instance, all his friends are taken away, so it may be fairer on him to walk him around to keep him occupied. In a case like this, he may just need some reassurance and stroking as you are leading him around.

For horses that continually bash their stable doors, there is a useful tip to save the door and the horses hooves. One idea is to have rubber matting by the door and then a plank of wood at the top of the inside of the door with some more rubber matting hanging down so that it would 'flap' if the horse were to knock it. Horses generally don't like this feeling. It's also worth having rubber matting on the floor by the door, to save wear and tear on the horse's legs and shoes, if he does still happen to scrape at all. Don't say, for instance, 'Naughty, naughty' as he scrapes the floor, or you will be teaching him that those words mean to scrape the floor.

Another short-term tip if you are holding a horse that is scraping is to raise your foot and let his front leg hit your boot. That usually surprises him just enough to stop him scraping for at least a minute. In that time you can then tell him how good he is for not scraping.

**SLOPS ALONG WHEN BEING LED UP**
To encourage a horse to lead up well, first you need to have taught him to yield to pressure, so that you are sure he fully understands the fundamentals of following the line. When leading a horse, it is important that you don't pull him tightly under the chin because that is actually going to encourage him to resist. You also need to understand very

clearly how your body language affects the horse. If the horse hesitates a little and you immediately turn round and look at him, it will often stop him completely. This is a very common mistake people make. Even once the basics have been established there are still some horses that, although they are technically 'leading' (in other words 'following'), just don't show themselves to advantage.

## THINGS YOU CAN DO TO HELP

Let's assume that you are entering a show class and you don't want your horse to walk or trot along as if he's on his last legs. In fact, you want him to sparkle and really catch the judge's eye. One thing is for sure: you need to do the opposite to the stable lad in the case study below. Remember, horses not only mimic other horses but they can mimic humans as well. They can certainly pick up your emotions. So the first thing you need to do is sparkle. Produce a feeling of anticipation and excitement. You need to inspire the horse.

You may be working with nervous horses and used to concentrating very hard on staying relaxed to keep a horse calm and lower his energy. Now you must do the opposite: you want to get the energy up, along the same lines as if you are sending a horse away in the round pen during a Join Up session (see pages 89-92). For a practice session, shake yourself out and feel yourself getting jittery. Keep this energy up and transmit it to the horse. Some people are naturally more this way inclined and some are better at calming. You need to work at it so that you can do either.

*Case study*

## 'SELLING RACES'

*In racing there are races called 'sellers' or 'selling races'. These are for the lower classes of racehorses who, if they win, will be offered for auction at a starting price of, say, £3000. If the bid goes over £3000, half the money goes to the racecourse and half to the owner. It's very rare that an owner actually wants to sell a horse in these circumstances; they are generally in there because it's the only type of race the horse can win. It's not unknown for owners to pay more than they have won on the prize money to buy the horse back again! On my father's 70th birthday his horse, Paddy, racing name 'Lucky Native', won a seller at Lingfield. It was all very exciting and then came the awful realization – Paddy would now be put up for auction. There was no way that Dad was going to let him go, so we waited to see how much the day was going to cost him. The lad led the horse into the ring and I have to say I have never seen such a sorry sight in my life. The lad walked with the speed and enthusiasm of someone going to the gallows. The horse followed with his head held down, trailing his feet and looking totally dejected. Who'd want a buy a horse like that? Nobody, thank goodness! When the auctioneer knocked down 'No Bid' they both bounced out of the ring like Tiggers.*

If you are still not getting the result you would like, some 'tricks of the trade' are given overleaf that you can try when training. Don't let your rivals see this!

1 Tie a plastic bag on to the end of a stick and just touch your horse on his hindquarters with it from behind your back when you want him to put in a little more effort. The idea is not to frighten him but just to enliven him a little.

2 Pairing the 'surprise' with a kiss noise means you can just use the kiss noise discreetly in the ring to wake him up. Don't make it obvious the plastic bag is to do with you and don't over use it. This works much better than a whip behind your back, which can sting, irritate or tickle. You don't want a horse that's looking backwards.

3 Use the plastic bag just enough, so that when he hears the kiss noise it encourages him to move with more energy. An alternative is positioning a friend 2 or 3m (7½ or 10ft) behind the horse, who then just scrapes the plastic bag on the floor as the horse sets off.

4 You can think about having something like pebbles in a can to shake a little as you go along to wake your horse up.

5 Another alternative is to place a friend with some feed in a bucket at the end of the run. What you want is a horse that trots along happily and expectantly, with his ears pricked forward – this can work very well.

### IN THE SHOW RING

When you are waiting in line and it is nearly your time to come out, into the show ring, start to ease your horse a little from side to side. If you have a chance to do some tight circles before the judge sees you (not always possible), that is ideal. It's always easier moving a horse at angles. First of all, you are going to stand your horse up for the judge. Your horse will place his feet perfectly because you have already worked through the Foundation Exercises. If he knows what the sound of a Polo wrapper means (see Using Food in your Training, pages 47-9), you can just rustle a small piece of paper to get him to prick his ears for the judge. You want to present a perfect 'picture'. You then lead him away from the judge at a walk. Hopefully, he is leading well at this stage but if he is starting to dawdle at all, you can make the kiss sound. You may choose to make your turn back sooner rather than later if he's dawdling along or wandering about. It's this turn before going into a trot where you have a very brief opportunity to enliven him again by just unbalancing him by moving him from side to side a little, making the kiss noise and starting him into the trot while he's still turning. The top show people make everything look effortless, but, make no mistake, they are actually working all the time.

Keep an eye on where the judge is looking as much as you can. It's unfair to expect your horse to stay continually alert with ears pricked the whole time – just reserve your 'tricks' for when the judge is looking.

If the horse is doing the wrong thing at any given time, always make it look as though as it were your mistake.

In show classes the fashion is for the horse to 'take you' along, so you've really got to get your horse to enjoy this. But let him know he can only play this game of 'trotting away with you' in quite specific circumstances.

With any of the methods described it is very important not to overuse them – that defeats the object. Most of all, remember showing is meant to be fun. Personally, I think it's a lot more fun if you prepare properly and give yourselves a chance of winning. It's a way of showing off your horse (who is the most beautiful in the world, no matter what any judge says) and spending quality time together. However, if you find yourself at any stage getting bad-tempered or frustrated with it, you need to rethink whether it's really for you. It's an expensive way to be miserable.

## NOT STANDING STILL TO MOUNT
### HOW THIS PROBLEMS STARTS

• The horse has never had it clearly and politely explained to him that he's supposed to stand still as the rider is getting on.
• The horse has never developed any trust in human beings.
• The horse is not standing four-square in the first place.
• The rider approaches the horse as if she is a predator about to eat him, giving him strong eye contact, square body positioning, arms outstretched and jerky movements.
• The rider digs her toe painfully in his side as she goes to get on.
• The rider has made it very uncomfortable for the horse as she 'hoicks' herself up and 'thumps' down into the saddle.
• The rider pulls the horse in the mouth as she gets on, or the horse senses that she might pull him in the mouth as she gets on.
• The rider always immediately rushes the horse off as soon as she hits the saddle, causing the horse to anticipate. This is particularly common with Arabs and any of the more sensitive horses.
• The horse has soreness and discomfort somewhere.
• The equipment used is uncomfortable, so the horse becomes sore and uncomfortable if he can't deter the rider from getting on.
• The horse has experienced some traumatic experience at some stage of his life and so panics when the rider goes to get on.

A key point, which runs through all these lessons, is the rider's expectation of what are normal manners. Some people do not realize that it is reasonable to expect your horse to stand perfectly still as you get on him and to wait for you to ask him to set off – just as some people allow themselves to be treated badly by other people because they haven't been brought up to believe they are worth more. In racing yards it is normal for you to receive a 'leg up' on to the racehorse as he walks along. This is how it is accepted that you mount these very fit, sensitive animals. However, there was a period of time when I worked in racing that I used to be left on my own to ride horses out in the afternoon. As I'm not particularly athletically inclined, each of the horses had to stand perfectly still by a carpenter's bench for me to get on, and every single horse stood and waited perfectly. It became the new, 'oh, this is how we do things round here' approach. Neither the horses nor I thought this was anything unusual until someone would come around and say, 'You can't get on racehorses like that!' Remember, horses can become creatures of habit very easily. If you just keep setting up good habits, very soon they'll make it their accepted way of doing things.

### THINGS YOU CAN DO TO HELP

When dealing with a mounting problem nowadays, this is how I'll tackle it, using the following steps:

1 Join Up (see pages 86-107) with the horse first. This enables me to have a good look at the horse and learn more about him, at the same time as starting to develop a bond with the horse and gaining his trust and respect.

2 I will also work with the horse to be sure he is perfectly happy with me touching and stroking him all over, massaging out any areas of tension. If you haven't reached this stage you're likely to be in for a pretty 'hairy' time once you do get on!

3 I also make sure he understands about yielding to pressure and how to place his feet as requested. (See earlier chapters.)

I went through the above steps with Elmo, who had been rescued by Lisa Bradley from being badly treated and handled by his previous owner (see page 151). Elmo was a beautiful grey Arab, who would either rear or charge off in panic if anyone tried to get on him. When he first arrived with Lisa, he was suffering from rainscald, a heavy-worm burden, mudfever, thrush in his hooves and an open wound on his face where a nylon headcollar had been left on too tight. Elmo's case is particularly memorable to me, partly because he was featured on the BBC

TV series I'm involved with and partly because of the enormous level of fear he showed, although being perfectly amiable in every other way. Elmo stayed with Ian and Sandy Vandenberghe in Oxfordshire. There were a number of different methods we used with Elmo as well as quite a few different people being involved – myself, Ian, Sandy, Grant Basin, Linda Ruffle, Wendy Mutch, Lisa – and this was in addition to the many students who were on the courses around that time.

## USING DIFFERENT METHODS

Human egos being what they are, we often love to argue that the 'A method' is far superior to 'B method', and 'I support such and such a trainer so I could never go along with the "C method."' Naturally, if any of these methods support cruelty and cause additional fear to the horse, it is right not to want anything to do with them. However, something that is perfect for one horse may not be right for another. All methods have the potential for being good or bad, depending on the skill and the intention of the people that are using them. Certainly, go with the method that appears the simplest and has worked most consistently for you but don't discount alternative ideas if you don't feel you are making the progress you'd expect.

You have to look at the reasons why the problem started. Is it lack of training? Fear? A rider problem? It's a good idea to look at the rider getting on another horse to see if you notice whether she is making the horse uncomfortable. Check to see how she approaches the horse – is it as a friend or a foe? Whether he or she gets on in the traditional English way facing the hindquarters and swinging round or the Western style of mounting facing forwards, it's important to check that the rider's toe isn't digging into the horse's side.

Consistently getting on from the ground from the same side is going to pull the saddle out of alignment sooner or later – and also the horse's back. So having a leg up is a good method but it is important that you know your horse will stand still by a mounting block for times when there is nobody else around. If the problem is fear based, your first obligation is to gain your horse's trust. Try to make every interaction between you a positive one. A method that will help your horse get over his fear and apprehension, and which helped Elmo a great deal, was just tying him in the barn area while we were working there. He'd have a haynet to keep him occupied. He would be fully tacked up and there would be a bale of straw beside him; every now and again I would go over to him, give him a stroke, climb on to the straw bale, give him a stroke on the other side and then climb down again. To start with, this made Elmo very fearful, but before long he was ignoring me, feeling totally confident that I wasn't going to hurt him. Now he was far more interested in his hay.

## GETTING A HORSE'S CONFIDENCE

Once you have gained the horse's confidence and you are sure the exercise isn't making him uncomfortable, or if you are just starting with a horse that doesn't know any better, an important step is to test if you are able to control his feet, as described in the Foundation Exercises (see pages 58-73).

1 A good way to check that he is standing firm is to give a slow pull on the stirrup leather nearest you, which will cause him to balance himself. You don't need to get on him just yet, but you should be able to manoeuvre your horse backwards and forwards or around, just as in the exercises you've been practising, and place him in just the position that you would like him.

2 You can climb up on your mounting block, and if he doesn't stand still, put those feet of his back to work – not aggressively, of course, but backwards, forwards, bending backwards each way, backwards, forwards again – and then offer him the opportunity to just stand.

3 Take a breath, give him a nice stroke and stand on the mounting block again and stroke him and tell him how good he is. If he moves off at any time, put him to work again. The first couple of times he stands, just get straight down again and go round the front to pet him.

4 Gradually, as he gets better, you can progress; stroke him on the opposite side, put a foot in the stirrup, stand up in the stirrup. The person who does this part of the work needs to be experienced, calm and athletic. If that's not you, then find the right person to help you. From time to time, get right down again and go to the front to tell him how good he is. By the time you actually do get on, he will be wondering what the fuss was about. It is very important now you are up there to just sit for a while – at least for a few minutes. So many of us are in such a rush all the time we can't blame our horses for getting more and more like us.

5 You can make the job much easier for yourself by just working initially in a corner so the horse has less scope for wandering around. You may like someone to hold the horse until he is really relaxed. There are many 'simplification' techniques that some people feel they can't do because it would somehow be 'cheating': 'But of course he'll stand still if you put him there!' Remember that in your training sessions you want to make the right thing easy for the horse to do, so he can quickly get the benefits of your rewards. As soon as he understands what it is you want, you'll be able to get on any time, any place, anywhere.

## Case study

# ELMO'S JOIN UP

*Our first plan with Elmo was to 'restart' him; doing a Join Up first of all to see if we could gain his trust and observing him in this process to see what it told us about how he was feeling about the human race and life in general. Lisa had already told me that she had done a great deal of lunging with Elmo in the time she'd had him to start to build some muscle on him and teach him voice commands. She said that to start with he'd been difficult to keep out and kept wanting to come in to her but she'd persisted until he gradually got the idea of staying out. Horses that have been brought on like this can be quite tricky to communicate with through the Join Up system because they've learned to 'switch off' to the visual signals from the handler. Elmo was no exception; coupled with his typical high Arabian head carriage always angled to look outside the pen, I could see this wasn't going to turn out to be a copybook Join Up. I persisted in gently encouraging him round the pen in either direction. I seemed to have some attention, judging by his inside ear; it was just the rest of his anatomy that was missing – eyes, head, body were all focused outside the pen. After the second turn I really took the pressure off, letting him even walk a step or two to give him the space to give the head-lowering sign. The head-lowering posture puts a horse at his most vulnerable, similar to a dog lying on his back or a human being with their arms up. It's not a gesture that can or should be forced at all. It's a gesture that is invited, by taking pressure off and allowing the horse to see he is dealing with someone reasonable and fair. Elmo soon lowered his head as invited but with such an air of 'I'm just sniffing the ground actually, so don't you go thinking anything's changed between us' it was hard to know if we were really making progress or not. My invitation was ignored, although he did slow to a halt and gaze into the far, far distance outside the pen. As usual, poor human eyesight and poor human imagination can never really fathom what's so interesting in those most distant fields. I just went up to him and gave him a stroke. I took him into the middle and spent plenty of time stroking and rubbing him; I then let him go and walked round and he stayed with me. Success? A bond developing? Maybe. At least a starting point from which to work. It was clear that Elmo wasn't going to be a push-over, though, and when you hear of some of his former treatment, nobody had the right to expect him to be any different.*

*We also spent some time putting a dummy on and off his back, long-lining him around the paddocks and teaching him to head lower on request to control his 'panic attacks'. He became so good that within a few weeks Lisa, his owner, could easily get on and off with no worry at all, right in the middle of an open field. People exclaimed, 'It's a miracle with that horse – so what was it that actually cured him?' The only answer can be, 'the magic is in the mix'. Putting all the ingredients together with a big dose of love for horses can have outstanding results. While some of the work we did may have had more impact than other parts, it all blended together to give the horse positive attention. We continued to learn about him and it let him know we cared and were there for him.*

### THINGS YOU CAN DO TO HELP

If your horse hasn't been handled enough, or isn't happy with you round his head, it is because you haven't completed your Foundation Exercises. If that is the case then go back to these exercises, but if it's just the sight of the syringe that upsets him, then you need to get him used to an old worming syringe. Once you've done that you can start preparing the horse to take the wormer in the back of his throat. At no stage do you want to start a battle.

1 First of all gently handle the horse's head all over. Check that you can easily open the horse's mouth by inserting your thumb upwards in his mouth and pressing his gum in the gap in his teeth where the bit always sits.

2 Next start to stroke his nose gently with the worming syringe. If he reacts negatively in any way to this, make sure you are holding it discreetly in your hand to start with before making it more obvious. Just spend a couple of nights making it part of your grooming routine.

3 When the horse is perfectly used to this, you may like to put some honey on the end of the syringe and put it in his mouth for a second or two, then pull it out (you don't want him to start chewing it). Let him register it was actually rather nice.

*Case study*

## HORSES LEARN BY ASSOCIATION

*I was at a horseman's clinic in 1998 and as always there was much of interest and 'food for thought'. However, I must admit I didn't agree with the trainer on one point. A member of the audience told the trainer, 'I held my horse while he was being castrated last year and ever since then the horse doesn't seem to like me very much!' There were roars of laughter from the audience and the trainer dismissed her concerns as all in her imagination. I went away thinking that her story didn't seem so unlikely at all. I've heard farmers say that they don't stay around with any of their bulls when they are having rings through their noses because they don't want the bull to associate it with them. Obviously, if your horse needs you, you should be there for him, but I would advise you to try and stay away when anything unavoidably unpleasant or painful is happening to your horse, if you can help it. I know of a horse that grew vicious with his lady owner because his castration operation went wrong and she had to come in and inject him every day. He was much happier with men ever afterwards. You hear of quite a few horses that 'don't like men' and if their early unpleasant experiences were with a male vet or a male farrier, you can understand how that's happened and, of course, it can also happen in reverse.*

*Case study*

# CELINA, A FOUR-YEAR-OLD WARM-BLOOD MARE

*I first met Celina when I went to the breeder to view another horse. I went to stroke her, and the owner warned me that she would try to attack me if I touched her, which she did. A week later the owner telephoned me and asked if there was any way I could help her because otherwise Celina was going to be sent for slaughter. I can't deny this horse was not easy but we succeeded in helping her and she is ridden today like most other horses. We don't know all her history but, as with many horses, I'm sure she had good reason to protect herself and be suspicious. But we have come a long way with her as she had a lot of physical problems that needed to be overcome, including problems with her teeth.*

*Because of her delicate temperament, the task of rasping her teeth was rather difficult. Having her sedated by injection was out of the question as she wouldn't let the vet near her.*

*I telephoned Pia Kaj, who is an equine dental technician in Denmark and has also done some of the Intelligent Horsemanship courses with Kelly, and I asked her to help me. We managed to do a light job on the left side, but Celina wouldn't let Pia in the right side.*

*Now, Celina has a thing about cinnamon cakes so we decided to dip the rasp in some cinnamon. After a short while using the cinnamon and advance/retreat training, she was allowing the rasp in her mouth. When she had done this a few times without throwing her head in the air, we decided to end the session. Next time Pia was around we had another go. Celina was less defensive this time and we managed to examine her teeth properly and put on a mouth gag without much resistance. Pia suggested that I worked with the handle of an old washing-up brush (a smooth and round handle), imitating the movement of the rasp. We also made sure she kept finding the taste of cinnamon. Having done this a few times a week for three weeks we were then able to remove the sharp edge on her teeth.*

**INTELLIGENT HORSEMANSHIP RECOMMENDED ASSOCIATE MAJ-BRITT CARTER**

4 When the time comes to administer the wormer for real, make sure you have everything prepared, and he has his headcollar on ready.

5 Finally, mke sure he is not eating at the time. (How many times have I put wormer in a horse's mouth, neatly and efficiently, only to have it all fall out with a big clump of hay in his mouth? I don't even want to think about it.)

## DENTISTRY

Many of the same issues described above for a trip to the vet apply to dentistry. I hope you enjoy the case study from Maj-Britt Carter in Denmark given above – it illustrates the perfect way of overcoming an all-too-common problem.

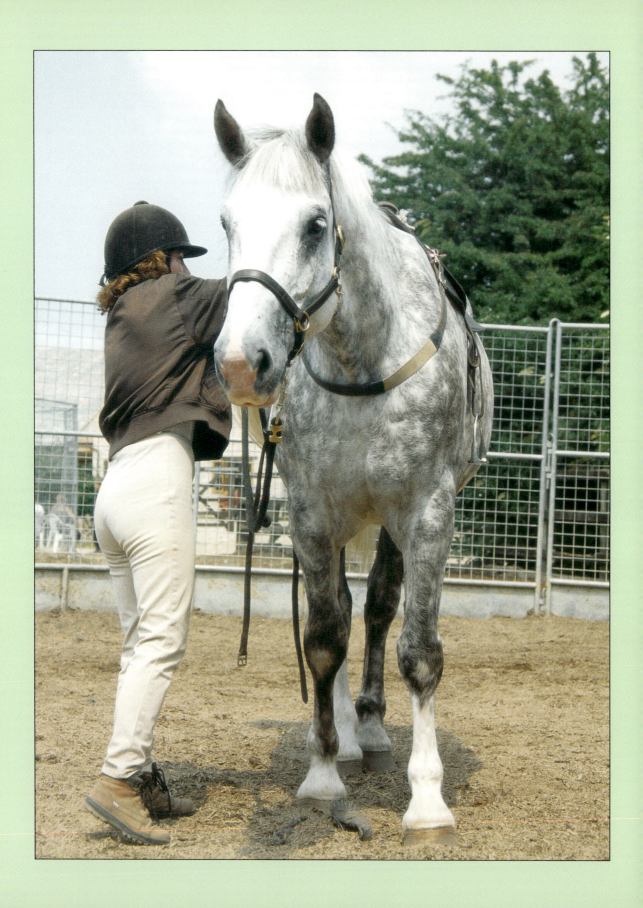

# *brushed and ready*
# TO GO

It's amazing how inconsiderate people can be to horses' sensitivities. My father tells me that there were countless numbers of savage horses before the war. Horses were fed large amounts of grain and stabled 23 hours a day and as labour was cheap they were subjected to incredible vigorous grooming routines for as much as a couple of hours a day, while their heads were chained high. With handling methods generally harsher in many ways, it drove some of the horses literally quite mad, and they got to hate people coming near.

This shouldn't be the case nowadays. Grooming should be a pleasant, invigorating experience for a horse. 'Skin brushing' has even proved health-giving for humans as well (marvellous for cellulite). If a horse resents the brushes, first check out what he's like with just your hands. The strokes you use should be firm and even – not 'ticklish' or tentative ones, as these are likely to irritate him more. Once he's comfortable with your hands, he should then be comfortable with the brushes. If he reverts to making faces or displaying unhappy behaviour once the brushes are introduced, it may be the brushes are too harsh for his sensitive skin, or it could be he has bad memories of when they were used before. Whatever the reason, it's important to ensure he finds the grooming process totally comfortable in the future.

It's not fair to expect a horse with sensitive skin to stand while a dandy brush is scratched over him, particularly on his most sensitive areas like under his belly and around his head. I prefer using a dry water brush for most grooming – it's far more comfortable for the horse. You may need to start grooming him with just a folded stable rubber to regain his confidence if he has really grown to resent any brushes. If mud is a big concern you may decide to have your horse rugged up when turned out, to keep him clean. (It goes without saying you'd have him rugged up if you were at all concerned about him being cold.) If the horse is totally caked in mud, sponging with warm water may be the best solution. Removing dried-on mud can be painful for a sensitive

**WELL GROOMED**
**GROOMING SHOULD BE A**
**PLEASURE FOR A HORSE.**

horse. If you want to go out for a ride, you may have to swallow your pride and only clean the areas where the tack would rub to avoid wetting the horse all over. Sometimes removing heavy mud is a process that needs to be done over several days.

## PUTTING ON RUGS

Some horses find having their rugs put on uncomfortable. The way to approach this with a young horse or older horse that needs particularly tender treatment is to fold the rugs over carefully to start with. Place the rugs over the bottom of his neck and gradually unfold. Do not let the buckles on the girth straps fall down and knock his shins. If a horse pulls his rug off at night more than once, he is clearly telling you he is not comfortable wearing it. Do not find ways of forcing him to wear something uncomfortable all night. Can you imagine having to go to sleep every night in an uncomfortable coat? It could be torture. Consider finding a more comfortable rug that he will like, otherwise leave it off – he was probably telling you he was too hot anyway.

## SENSITIVITY TO PICKING UP FEET AND LEG HANDLING
### HOW THIS PROBLEM STARTS

• The horse is unhandled and so his legs are sensitive to being touched.
• Someone may have provoked this sensitivity and when the horse went down on the floor because of it, they may have thought he was being deliberately evasive and not dealt with the issue correctly.
• The horse has never been taught how to place his feet as requested.
• The horse has never had it clearly and politely explained to him that he's supposed to pick his feet up immediately and calmly on request.
• The horse hasn't learned to lead, back up and respect human space.
• People have taken an aggressive attitude with the horse, which has frightened him and turned him off the very idea of anyone handling his feet.
• In the early stages of training, when the horse hasn't known what is expected, people have 'grappled' with his feet, holding them far too high.
• People have held his feet up high, then suddenly 'dropped' them, unnerving him.
• The handler hasn't checked to

**PICKING UP THE FORELEGS**
I HAVE TAUGHT PIE THAT WHEN
I PRESS HIS SHOULDER HE
SHOULD PICK UP HIS FOOT.

see the horse is standing in a balanced position before asking for his feet to come up.

• There is a physical problem: for example, soreness in the shoulder area would affect picking up the front feet. An upward fixation of the patella is a common problem in young and unfit horses especially those with straight hock and stifle conformation. These conditions make it sometimes impossible for the horse to pick up his hindfeet. The patella is the equivalent of our kneecap and one of three bones that are part of the horse's stifle. If the horse will let you touch his leg but seemingly refuses to bend it, you may see if he improves with more exercise and building up. If this condition is unfamiliar, consult a vet.

## THINGS YOU CAN DO TO HELP

1 You can see that the first four problems will be solved by doing the Foundation Exercises (see pages 58-73). Do remember that training your horse is not your farrier's job, it is your responsibility. Your farrier's job is to do the best possible work on your horse's feet. If your horse has a real phobia about shoeing, it would be worth making a deal with your farrier and asking him to come over at least a couple of times and give your horse some feed out of a bucket and stroke him all over and leave it at that. I am regularly told about horses that 'don't like men'. This is often due to the horse not enjoying his early experience with a male farrier or vet (of course, there are far more female farriers and vets now); it doesn't necessarily mean that they were unfair or unkind – only that the horse found it unpleasant and isn't keen to repeat it.

2 While it is necessary for horses to have regular footcare and trimming, it is not always necessary for horses to wear shoes. You could explore different alternatives. With correct and regular trimming, optimum living conditions and careful conditioning of the hoof to cope with different types of ground, many horses can be happy, healthy and sound without ever being shod. In an ideal world, let your farrier come over to do some of the other horses in the yard while your youngster looks on. You can then make your farrier a nice cup of tea and cunningly ask, 'Would you mind casually stroking this horse while we're chatting here?'

PICKING UP THE HINDLEGS IF YOU ARE UNSURE OF A HORSE, TRY IT THIS WAY. APPARENTLY IT'S LESS PAINFUL TO BE KICKED ON THE BACK OF THE KNEE THAN THE FRONT.

## LEG-HANDLING TIPS

Balancing on three legs and being deprived of his natural flight response is most definitely not natural for a horse. For them to give their feet over easily to us is a privilege we have to earn, as in all our dealings. The way to proceed with a horse that has never had his feet picked up, or with a 'difficult' case, is the same:

1 Work in a safe, enclosed area, a minimum of 6 x 6m (20 x 20ft), where the horse can move away from you if he is worried. It's when they feel 'trapped' that they feel the need to strike out to protect themselves. First of all concentrate on petting and stroking all the areas that the horse is happy with you touching.

With all the exercises I describe further on about leg handling, you can choose to have an assistant to hold the horse. The assistant needs to place himself or herself on the same side as you are working and be ready to pull the horse's head round quickly to swing his hindquarters away from you if he is going to kick out. If an assistant isn't available these exercises can be carried out quite well alone with you holding the line yourself. You don't need to have a tension in the line but you don't want more than 8 or 10cm (3 or 4in) of slack. If the horse looks like kicking out, you need to bring his head towards you so his back end moves away.

2 Using the back of your hand initially, start where he is happy and gradually work with the back of your hand down to the 'ticklish area'. Do your best to remove your hand before the horse starts to protest. Remember, we are working to overcome some of his basic fears, i.e. the removal of the flight option. Plus the horse needs to learn how to overcome his sensitivity to touch and you should help him to work out how to balance.

3 Make sure you can touch and rub the whole leg before you attempt to pick up the leg. For the first attempt at picking up the front leg, just put your hand behind the horse's knee and give a few little pulls forward to release the stay apparatus of the leg. This is the part of the horse that means he can rest and sleep while he is standing up. Just hold on to the leg for a couple of seconds before gently replacing the foot on the floor.

4 With the hindleg on the nearside, holding the line just a little slack in the rope but ensuring it's not down too low, put your left hand on his hip and run the other hand right down from his hindquarters to his hindleg, just above the back of the fetlock – i.e. don't just grab at his foot as this is a sure way to get kicked.

It's our non-threatening attitude built on a trust-based relationship that's so important.

*Case study*

# THE EXPLOSIVE ARABIAN MARE

*I should think I have now dealt with more remedial horses for shoeing than most farriers! The latest horse I had was a grey, eight-year-old Arabian mare. She was used for endurance riding, so it was clearly essential that she wore shoes, but to fit them she had always been heavily sedated. Two farriers were unwilling to deal with her any more as they reported her to be dangerous, aggressive and explosive. Her way of kicking, biting and rearing during even basic leg handling by the owner was very dangerous.*

*On arrival (the mare had to be sedated to be loaded and travel), she was excited and very alert. The owner mentioned that she would take several days to settle in to her new environment. This, however, wasn't the case as she settled within minutes, to the owner's astonishment. The next thing I noticed was the mare did not respect the handler's personal space. After a Join Up (see pages 86-107), where I looked to see if the horse was sound in movement, and a follow up, we proceeded. I tested the mare to see how she reacted to me lifting a front leg. I ran my hand down from the shoulder to her forearm and she sunk to her knees. This told me that she was very sensitive to touch – a common feature with Arabs. It meant I had to desensitize her legs before I could ask to pick them up. To do this, I used a long dummy hand to touch a non-sensitive part of the horse before moving the arm towards a more sensitive area, but removing the dummy hand before the horse moved away. I then reintroduced the dummy hand to another leg region, going from non-sensitive to sensitive areas. The removal of the dummy hand is very important before the horse moves away. The horse may flinch but you can continue as long as he returns to a calm outlook; I worked around the horse, touching the legs in turn and gradually going down them. Having completed that, we called it a day.*

*The next day I repeated the exercise and progress was achieved much more quickly. Then I proceeded to pick up her legs. The front ones she struck out and the hind ones she kicked out. This needed a training halter to remedy the ingrained fear. After making sure the horse understood the pressure and release of the training halter, we proceeded. The most important aspect of this behavioural training is the release, not the pressure. When the horse did anything untoward when I was lifting up the leg, I then applied immediate pressure to the halter, and when the horse came off the pressure, I released my grip on the halter. Again, when I achieved some progress with one leg, I proceeded to the next one rather then concentrating on the same leg all the time. As soon as the horse understood me, the problems disappeared.*

*The next stage was the farrier. I held the mare in a training halter and went over the same procedure as before but took less time, just using the dummy hand and doing some pressure and release work. The farrier cold-shod one front leg and one hindleg and only some minor pressure and release work was needed. She was put away while the farrier shod another horse. Then, after a ten-minute break, he finished the mare with no problems. The break in the middle was essential to make sure she didn't get tired, bored or irratated. Finished result: a shod horse with no sedation and aggravation. A job well done by the team!*

**INTELLIGENT HORSEMANSHIP RECOMMENDED ASSOCIATE IAN VANDENBERGHE**

5 Gently give several little pulls forward. When the horse gives his leg, hold on for a couple of seconds before releasing it. If you are working with a strange horse who may just kick out, another way to approach the hindleg is with your back to the horse's body. On the near-side, hold the line with your right hand and really stretch your left arm out to stroke down and pick up the back leg. I've heard it's less painful to be kicked on the back of the knee than the front – though really I'd prefer not to experience either.

6 Often people start to touch a horse's leg and when he moves off they stop touching the leg. You can imagine the horse interpreting that as, 'If I just move away she stops touching my leg – that must be what I'm meant to do!' This doesn't mean you should battle against all odds to hang on to a horse's leg but it does mean that you should try in the training to remove yourself just before the horse does anything you don't want. You initially make the reward your moving away. By doing this you can gradually gain his trust, and you can then move a bit lower down the leg each time.

## PRAISE IS IMPORTANT

Reward must be given for a positive outlook by the horse; use plenty of praise to build the trust. This method is ideal for the young horse and can be repeated on a daily basis so that more and more is achieved.

Each time you have any little success, work with a different leg. If you feel the horse may kick out or you need some extra confidence, just get someone to give you a hand. An artificial hand as seen in the photo (see opposite) can easily be made up with a glove and a sleeve on a stick. If the horse kicks at the hand, you don't need to worry; just put the hand back in place immediately. This also saves you being bent over for too long a period of time.

Another method that works with a horse that really kicks out behind, is putting a soft cotton rope round the back leg, and keeping yourself safe, allowing the horse to kick and fuss with the rope as he wishes and then petting him when he stops fussing with it.

• The first goal is not to pick up the horse's feet, but for the horse to be completely happy with you touching right down all his legs.
• Make sure the horse is standing in a balanced position before you start so he is going to be comfortable to do as you ask.
• Once this is accomplished, you can work on getting each leg a little higher, cleaning them out and moving them forward as if for the far-rier. When you first want to hold the front legs up a little longer, curl one of the legs over and just hold the toe lightly. If the horse protests and hops a little, just gently stay with him and as soon as he relaxes put the toe down and give him a stroke.

It's important to stand in close to the horse without touching his flank, so he won't be able to get any speed and power up if he were to kick at you. Boxers know that if they can't avoid a punch, it's best to go into the punch which will take the force from the blow.

**WHO'S THAT IN THERE?**
**(OVERLEAF)**
HORSES SHOULD BE ENCOURAGED TO HAVE HIGH SELF-ESTEEM. WHEN PIE FIRST CAUGHT SIGHT OF HIMSELF IN A MIRROR HE'D NEVER SEEN ANYTHING SO BEAUTIFUL.

• You can hold up the toe of the back foot as well.

Once the horse starts to understand what you want him to do, he will soon get into the routine and will pick his feet up in response to you just leaning in on him a little; your elbow will be behind his knee, and either simply squeezing gently just above the fetlock joint or even just touching there.

## HORSES WITH VERY HEAVY FEET

This doesn't necessarily mean shire horses although it could do. You get some horses that really lean on you when you pick up their feet or else firmly 'plant' them on the ground, while you are sweating and straining as you pull at their leg. I would advise before you do your back permanent damage that you ask an assistant to help and possibly use a training halter. Ask the assistant to help you move the horse so that you can 'catch' the leg as it comes off the ground as he takes a step backwards. Gradually, once you've timed it right a few times, the horse should gain more idea of what you want.

As is often the case with horses, the 'five-minute rule' applies: 'If you go in with the attitude that you've got all day, it will probably take you all day. If you go in with the idea that you need all day, it will probably only take you five minutes'. Ian Vandenberghe, who teaches leg handling at our Intelligent Horsemanship courses, says he has found his progress even faster when he is lecturing students at the same time because he is constantly stopping to explain things. This takes the pressure to perform off the horse.

**NEED A HAND?**
IAN VENDENBERGHE USES THIS SIMPLEST OF DEVICES TO HELP INCREASE THIS HORSE'S CONFIDENCE IN HAVING HER LEGS TOUCHED.

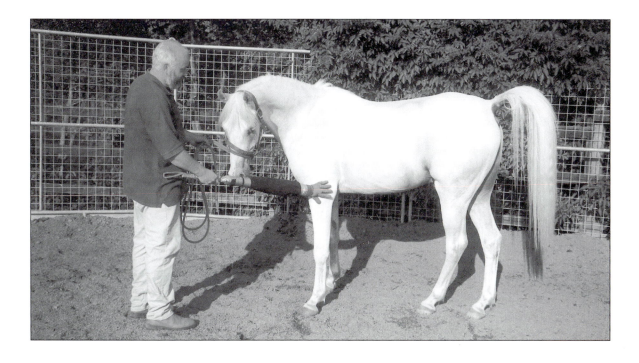

## DISLIKES HAVING HIS MANE PULLED
### HOW THIS PROBLEM STARTS

• The horse dislikes having large chunks of his hair pulled out by the roots – not too surprisingly.

Now attend! You are learning from a woman who knows pain. Eyebrows, legs, underarms – you name it – I've had hair pulled out by the roots in those places. I have never known it to be pleasant. Done by a different person and in different surroundings it could be defined as 'torture'. Some horses appear to have no problems with having their mane being pulled out by the roots. Perhaps it is because the person doing the pulling is particularly adept. Certainly in my own experience the right beauty therapist can make the difference between the process being merely uncomfortable as opposed to absolutely agonizing. It could be, of course, that the horse is just particularly obliging.

### THINGS YOU CAN DO TO HELP

1 One thing is for certain, if you are going to pull a mane painlessly you will need very strong fingers that can quickly pull out four or five strands of hair at a time. Going for large chunks of hair, in an effort to 'get the job over with', is bound to result in the horse not wanting to

A CLASS ACT

NICOLE GOLDING INTRODUCES THE CLIPPERS. NOTE THE HORSE LICKING AS HE THINKS ABOUT IT.

*Case study*

# A RACEHORSE WITH MANE PROBLEMS

*On our October 2000 tour, for the first time ever we took a horse that 'wouldn't have her mane pulled'; a yearling racehorse filly, whose owner adamantly stated, 'You won't get this done. We can't even comb it!' The filly came into the arena looking like some wild creature with a long straggly mane containing various knots and twists. I took her into the arena and I gently worked with the Solocomb™ for a minute or so. As soon as she realized it wasn't going to hurt, the filly relaxed completely and then she went out with IH Recommended Associate Karen Cunningham during the interval for further 'smartening up' in the corner of the arena. Various members of the public went over and watched to see how it was done and to see how unconcerned the filly was now. When the break was over and everybody was back in their seats, Karen brought her back in for a short 'parade'. The filly had by now completely shed her wild-child look and instead we had a real thoroughbred.*

*Sometimes the 'little problems' can be just as frustrating to people (and horses) as some of the bigger ones. I hope we help people consider that there's so often a different route to take – sometimes too simple to seem true.*

know about the process ever again. Pulling out a few hairs every now and then as you are tidying your horse up can mean it never has to become an issue.

2 Another idea to make it more comfortable to pull a mane, apart from speed and dexterity, is to lay a comfortably hot towel on the area to open the pores.

3 Endorphins act as natural painkillers and these are raised after 20 minutes of aerobic exercise, so it makes sense to do any pulling straight after exercise.

4 Remember, pain requires concentration so anything that distracts the horse is a good thing.

5 I've heard of people who pull the mane from the opposite side they want it to lie (usually the offside). The horse is usually less sensitive to the hair being pulled

### BEWARE OF CLOVE OIL

I have heard of clove oil being recommended as a local anaesthetic for humans and for pulling manes on horses. If you consider this option, you need to be very sure about the quality of oil you are buying. There have been reports of a variety of unpleasant side effects, including open sores, puffiness and scabbing. Some people have suffered severe burns after using the oil on their skin. Cloves contain a major irritant called 'eugenol'. The area of the plant that contains the least amount of this natural chemical is in the buds. The buds of cloves also produce a good amount of oil, but not surprisingly they can only be harvested at a certain time of the year. This causes some (greedy) growers and manufacturers to substitute oil that is extracted from the stems and leaves of the clove plant. Be careful as this creates a very toxic oil that can result in burns to the skin.

out from the top of the mane. You will find, if you practise first on your eyebrows, that it is much less painful if you pluck smoothly in the direction that the hair is already growing. The same concepts apply to tail pulling: if your horse finds it painful but a neat tail is necessary for show classes, learn how to plait tails beautifully.

Horses don't need to have their manes pulled for their own sakes and you may consider, rather than putting your horse through any discomfort, to let him go 'au naturel'. Long manes can look wonderful, but can be impractical for some sports if the reins get caught up in the flowing locks and so will need plaiting.

6 Mane pulling may well be considered archaic before very long, anyway, with the advent of the very successful 'humane mane pullers' which are now on the market. Many people swear by them nowadays, saying they get none of the ill-effects of cutting the mane, such as over-thickness or the give-away geometrically straight look, favoured by Vidal Sassoon in the 1960s. Even with a Solocomb™ (see box, left) you still have to have patience and finesse, however, taking very few mane hairs at a time and trimming close to the roots. I would certainly recommend this method with any horse that found mane pulling to be painful or unpleasant.

> **THE SOLOCOMB™**
> This is a plastic comb with a blade in it. You comb out the mane, backcomb as close to the roots as you can and then press a 'trigger' on the handle which makes the blade come across the teeth of the comb and cut the few strands of hair left. Use the Solocomb™ to backcomb the hair the same way as you would using a pulling comb, and while gripping it firmly, simply press the lever on top of the handle and the hair is clipped by high-quality steel blades. This comb can be used on manes and tails.

### CLIPPING

Clipping should not be considered until you have done the Foundation Exercises (see pages 58-73) thoroughly, and are sure that your horse is relaxed and happy to accept the touching all over and head-lowering exercises. Now your task is to 'define the problem', i.e. work out exactly what it is the horse doesn't like about clipping. Is it the sound of them? Is it the feel of the clippers? Is it the trail of electric cord? Or is it something else entirely?

### HOW THIS PROBLEM STARTS

• The horse has never been taught to accept clippers in the first place.
• Someone has just gone in to a young horse with a pair of clippers and expected him to stand dutifully still. When he hasn't, it's become a big issue which, with no proper plan of introducing the clippers, has only got worse over time.

*Case study*

# BLAKE, THE BIG SHIRE HORSE

*Blake was the biggest horse my partner, Adam Goodfellow, and I had ever dealt with. He'd been burned on the flank by a pair of clippers, and since that time couldn't be clipped without serious sedation. His bulk made this drugging a particularly dangerous option. Having established all the groundwork exercises, we decided to check his reaction to the clippers. He was in our largest stable, and we switched them on about 100m away from him, yet he still jumped to the back of his stable, and stood shaking. The clippers that came with him were very fast, and they would guarantee a smooth, close cut, but were noisy. We decided to borrow some quieter, cordless ones.*

*Blake wasn't a particularly food-motivated horse, but I found putting my electric toothbrush in a rubber bucket, and putting his food in another bucket on top of that, was a good start. It didn't take long before he would happily eat out of a noisy, vibrating food bowl.*

*The joy of using cordless clippers isn't just that the cord doesn't get in the way, it's also that they can be taken anywhere. We took Blake up to the school, and while one of us held him, the other stood at the far end of the school, with the clippers switched on. We then asked Blake to take a step towards the clippers, and as soon as he did, the person holding the clippers moved a step away. It was almost as if the clippers were frightened of Blake! It took about a week of three sessions a day to get him to the stage where he could tolerate the clippers being held about 3m (10ft) away from him, and to have them placed on his body while switched off.*

*With such big horses, there's no way I can hold them should they move away, so I make a rule: they can move backwards away from the clippers if they feel too frightened to stay close, but they will have to come forward again at some point. Under no circumstances can they run straight over the top of me, and if they try, I'll use the methods Kelly's described previously for getting a horse out of your space. Once they realize they can move backwards if needed, they'll take this option over barging through you.*

*Horses who are really frightened of clippers are unlikely to let you put the clippers on them while they're switched on. It's almost impossible to 'sneak' them on to the horse. However, I have a cunning ruse. I've found it enormously useful to switch on the clippers , turn them off, and then put them on the horse. Having turned them on, it might take a few minutes to put them on the horse, but if you stay patient and work quietly, you will succeed.*

*I keep doing this until I can put the clippers straight on the horse's body as soon as I've switched them off. At some point (it doesn't usually take long) I'll become confused, and end up switching them on, putting them on his body, and then switching them off. Celebration! Most horses notice, but at this point are not too worried. If you have a very violent reaction, return to putting them on while switched off. If the reaction is only mild, keep going, leaving them on for fractionally longer each time. This worked with Blake, and do you know the best thing about doing Blake? We didn't have to crouch down too low to do under his belly! We left his beautiful feathered legs on, but did the rest of his body all out. This is much easier than just doing the sensitive bits, as in a trace clip.*

**INTELLIGENT HORSEMANSHIP RECOMMENDED ASSOCIATE NICOLE GOLDING**

When you hear and see the results of some horses' clipping experiences you really can't blame them for being reluctant to face the clippers again. I have seen horses with scars from where the clippers have burned or cut them – it's appalling.

## THINGS YOU CAN DO TO HELP

1 A young horse should be introduced to clipping in a systematic fashion. First of all he should be very well handled and capable of doing all the Foundation Exercises (see pages 58-73) smoothly. In particular, being handled all over, head lowering and the positioning of the feet need to be perfect. If he is very strong, consider using a training halter.

2 If possible get him to stand and watch other horses while they are standing relaxed as they are being clipped. Do remember when clipping, that if the clippers are too hot to place on the back of your hand then they are too hot to go on your horse's skin. Horses are generally more relaxed if they can be clipped in their own stable. To avoid making too much mess you can always sweep most of the bedding to the side and have a rubber mat for him to stand on. It's advisable for him to have someone at his head to hold him initially. He can also have a haynet to help him relax while you are doing his body.

3 To test a horse's reaction to the noise of the clippers, turn them on outside the box to start with. If he is very frightened of the noise, it may be advisable to desensitize him to that first. You can, as previously suggested, have him around other horses being clipped. You can regularly turn the clippers on to let him get used to them. You can even, as one of my students did, make a tape recording of the clippers that she placed beside his manger as he was eating. Putting cotton wool in the horse's ears can help muffle the sound and is a good idea anyway if going round the head area as it stops hairs falling down their ears. Clippers are getting more sophisticated and quieter all the time; if the noise is a big problem for your horse, consider buying one of the latest models of clippers. Monty Roberts recommends using a hairdryer over them initially, on a non-heated setting. The cool breeze can be pleasant and gets them used to the noise and movement.

## IF THE HORSE IS FRIGHTENED OF THE FEEL OF THE CLIPPERS

After mimicking the clippers with a rubber curry comb or whatever (use your imagination), think about buying some moustache trimmers from a local electrical shop. What we are looking for is the mildest stimulus possible to start with so that we can gain the horse's confidence, and gradually build on it. I always encourage my students to be imaginative, and one of them (as explained in the case study described by Nicole

Golding on page 171) first started getting the horse used to the noise of the clippers with an electric toothbrush of all things.

First work the clippers all over the horse's body while they're switched off. Do make sure they are disconnected from the power supply – accidentally turning them on when neither of you is expecting it can be disastrous.

1 Once the horse is happy with the noise, you can get him used to the feel of the clippers by having them turned on, but not clipping. To start with, move the clippers in the same direction as the hair growth. When he accepts the clippers on him, you can try a small cut – move the clippers along the lie of the coat, then move them up a centimetre, and then move them down again. A lot of horses really notice the first feeling of the hair actually being clipped, but by taking off a really small amount at a time you can minimize the shock.

2 A lot of people start clipping at the shoulder because this is an easily accessible place, but remember, if other people have tried before you to clip the horse, he may already be suspicious of this area being clipped. Also, be sure to avoid any bony prominences to start with. If the horse is too worried to have the clippers on his body while they're switched on, even after you've done all the necessary foundation, desensitizing work, read through the case study above.

Remember: Be very patient, and don't push for too much, or you could undo all your good work so far. End each session as soon as you get even a small positive response, and when you return to the work, make sure you go back a stage or two, rather than trying to put the clippers straight on the horse.

## IF THE HORSE IS FRIGHTENED OF THE ELECTRIC CORD
I would suggest you work with a long rope to start with, working up to pulling it all over your horse's body and along the ground without him worrying. A short-term solution to bear in mind is that there are some very good cordless clippers available nowadays. However, your horse shouldn't be unnecessarily frightened of cords, ropes, wires and it is best to address the fear sooner rather that later.

## IN GENERAL
Be sure not to attempt to 'trap' your horse to accept anything that he perceives as unpleasant, such as clippers or injections. Work with him off a long line so if he jumps away he can only go about 2 to 3m (6 to 8ft). He will then meet the end of the line and immediately be asked back in again. Soon he will start to control himself and be less and less inclined to jump away.

# *all*
# DRESSED UP

## DISLIKES HEAD HANDLING

### HOW THIS PROBLEM STARTS

• The horse has never been taught to have his head handled.

• The horse has been hit around the head.

• The horse has had an 'ear twitch' used on him (a rope tightened round his ears to make him stand still – a stupid, dangerous practice).

• The horse has had his ear grabbed tightly to make him stand still (another short-sighted practice).

• The horse has ear mites or a fungal infection or some other medical reason for not wanting his ears touched.

The points made under the Foundation Exercises and the Additional Yielding Exercises – Comfort-Touching (see page 68) and Neck Flexing (see page 78) – are appropriate for improving your horse's opinion of head handling.

As a precaution get your vet to look in your horse's ears to check for parasites or a fungal infection. He may even be able to tell if there has been an infection in the past which could explain the present problems. Once the vet has quickly carried out the appropriate checks you will know how to progress in the most effective way.

### THINGS YOU CAN DO TO HELP

Once you are sure pain isn't an issue then you can get on with the work of improving his reactions. I had three students once, who all worked together on a project to improve Cynthia, an extremely head-shy horse who wouldn't let you touch her ears at all. They each had a preferred method: one used Bowen (a very gentle soft-tissue massage technique); one used aromatherapy; and the other gave her Bach flower remedies. After four weeks I can happily report that Cynthia was perfect to handle all round her ears and head, she was happy to wear the crocheted

ALL DRESSED UP AND READY TO GO
A SMART TURN OUT DOESN'T HAVE TO BE FORMAL.

ear cover they made and was undisturbed by having a bridle put on. Three years later this continues to be the case (though admittedly she hasn't been wearing her crocheted ear cover on a regular basis; it's really something for special occasions – I'm sure you'd agree). Unfortunately, we have no idea which of the methods effected the cure – perhaps it was having three women constantly fussing around her head that was the deciding factor.

Again, it's probably a case of the 'magic being in the mix'. Although I will always try to give you the guidelines that will help you and your horse, remember that anything you do to increase your horse's trust and respect at any time is going to improve your relationship and increase your chances of success.

I know that a hard hat and strong footwear is advised for all exercises at the beginning of the book but I'd particularly recommend them in the case of not being able to touch the ears. The bigger the horse the more important protective clothing is. This is a job where patience is particularly important. There is nothing more trying to patience than a clout across the face or a horse jumping painfully on your foot. What you mustn't do is make a grab for the ear and try and 'hang on in there' until the horse gives up. This can be painful for you and the horse.

1 Work with slow, circular massaging movements in an area that the horse is comfortable with, as close as possible to the ears. Gradually move your massaging movements closer and closer to the ears.

2 If the horse resists, edge back a little bit until he accepts it again, then go into the area a little way once more. As I said earlier, patience is a crucial factor here and I advise that you put aside some specific time to work with your horse. You certainly don't want him to feel any tension from you. A good to prevent this happening is to have the radio on you and your horse's favourite station and 'chill out' as you massage away.

## MUSIC WHILE YOU WORK

Studies have shown that Baroque music, such as that by Bach and Vivaldi, can have a relaxing effect on horses and also increase learning in children and adults. For example, in 1993, experiments were carried out on school children in Wales who had a poor performance record, were disruptive and academically lacking. Mozart pieces were played in the classroom in a controlled experiment and it was found conclusively that the music had a positive effect, and improved not only the behaviour of the children, but also their academic achievement. Horse heart-rate monitors are available to assess the horse's reactions to different music, or alternatively you can take your horse's pulse. It's equally important for you to measure what effects different types of music have on you. If you are relaxed then your horse will be. Experiment with different music in your yard to see how it makes you feel. We tried some Acker Bilk, and you honestly do feel completely different! Note: Horses shouldn't be subjected to music constantly, and certainly not loud music.

3 Something that can help enormously is to 'accidentally' touch the ears whenever the opportunity arises. Quickly brush your hands lightly over the ears and then go back to doing unrelated things with your horse. This seems to work on a subconscious level. The horse hasn't had time to worry about it, but the message gets through that the ears are now a touchable area. The hairdryer technique described in Clipping (see page 172) may work in a similar way. The light breeze on the ears can feel pleasant to the horse, bringing a change of attitude.

It will help if your horse has done a Join Up (see pages 86–107) and you have created a strong bond with him before you start this exercise. It doesn't work to restrain a horse tightly to 'force' him to accept you. It instils a panic in him rather as it would in any of us if the dentist said, 'You are absolutely not allowed to move in this chair.' We know we are free to stop the dentist at any time. However, we are also aware that it is not acceptable for us to run into the reception area screaming and shouting and upsetting waiting clients. While a reasonable amount of freedom is to the benefit of the horse, I'm not convinced that the round pen method of working with your horse loose and sending him canter-ing round the pen every time he resists, is the kindest and most effective way either. I've heard of this working well, and yet I've also seen people work like this for long periods and only confuse and even distress the horse, as he starts to think that the human doesn't want him near at all.

## USING A MILD TRAINING HALTER

The theory of making it comfortable near you, and uncomfortable away from you, can be utilized more effectively, in my opinion, with the use of a mild training halter. As with the clipping or injecting scenarios, if you work in a round pen or any similar safe, enclosed area and the horse moves away, let him go a few steps until he meets the end of the rope you are holding and so makes himself feel some pressure from the hal-ter. Immediately and gently ask him back to you. Give him a stroke and some praise and then get back to your massaging. Quickly the horse realizes the boundaries – that he is absolutely free to move away, but not too far. You will even see him consciously thinking about it and making the decision not to move away.

Working in the way I've described means there is no reason to upset the horse at all and the training sessions can be kept to manageable amounts of time. All you need to ensure is that the session always fin-ishes on a positive note.

## PUTTING ON THE BRIDLE

There are some interesting ideas you can use in the stable, such as hav-ing strips of material hanging down in the stable and over the manger so the horse starts to get used to the idea of having things constantly touching his ears and so gets desensitized to them. You can see why having a vet check out the horse first is essential, though. If there was a medical condition it would be horribly unfair to subject the horse to this until he was completely cured.

When putting on the bridle, as discussed before in Rules of Training (see pages 26-57), it is helpful to define where the problem actually lies. Is it the ears, the mouth? Is the horse frightened of being touched around his head? Is it that your jacket is too tight, so that you are unable to reach your arms up higher and less clumsily? (I don't think these things up, you know – these are all things that have actually happened.) Assuming that the horse is now happy to be touched around the head and the neck and also that he accepts the head-lowering cues and head flexing as described in the Additional Yielding Exercises (see pages 74-85), let's first look at getting a bit in his mouth.

## PUTTING IN THE BIT

For this work I find a Happy Mouth or similar lightweight synthetic bit invaluable because if I make any mistake putting the bit in, it won't bang on the horse's teeth. Practise opening the horse's mouth, just to make sure that you are both proficient at it.

1 Stand on the left side of your horse's neck, take your right hand behind his jaw on to the bridge of his nose to keep him steady, and put your left thumb in the space between his teeth where his bit goes. Press gently upwards on his gum to open his mouth. Just have it open for a second or two and then let it close and tell him he's good. When you are proficient at that, then try opening it and putting the bit in at the same time – just the bit on it's own, no bridle attached. You could have a little honey or something sweet on the bit.

**OPEN WIDE**
TO ASK YOUR HORSE TO OPEN HIS MOUTH, PRESS GENTLY UPWARDS IN THE GAP BETWEEN HIS TEETH.

2 Before putting the bridle and bit on, stand on the left side of your horse's neck and, with the bridle in your left hand, bring your right hand round the back of his head and place it on the front of his face. Gently move it from side to side so that you can feel that he is comfortable to move with you, and yield to you.

*Case study*

# CUTTING OUT LUMPS

*Since studying Intelligent Horsemanship and then starting as a tutor on Kelly's courses, I have become more and more interested in looking at things from the horse's point of view and particularly in relation to how many 'behavioural problems' are in fact caused by the pain of an ill-fitting saddle. The importance of a well-made, well-fitting saddle cannot be overemphasized. As the one item of saddlery that transmits the rider's weight to the horse's back, it has the most profound impact on the horse's welfare. It's sadly all too common to see horses with significant saddle damage – white scars, big dips behind the withers, lumps and bumps – and a lot of people see these as being the normal result of riding. It really doesn't have to be this way. I think the worst example I've had of this yet was provided by a student who attended a course with us. Her horse had a few problems and had developed two lumps on his back, both on the same side, which just wouldn't subside. She had the saddle checked by two different fitters, both of whom proclaimed there was nothing wrong with the saddle. Her vet had a look at the lumps on the horse's back, and then took a look at the saddle, and also stated that the saddle wasn't the cause. He couldn't explain the lumps, but offered to cut them out surgically, which she said she'd go away and think about.*

*After listening to the saddle-fitting lecture given on Kelly's course, she contacted Kay Humphries with whom we all work closely. A good saddle fitter will be able to tell if a saddle is well-fitting, but without taking the panels off the saddle, it's impossible to tell what the saddle is like inside. Kay took the saddle apart, and found that the two small pieces of leather holding the D-rings in place were the cause: when the saddle was made, no one had smoothed these off, and over time these lumps had affected the horse's back – even though the panels were between them and the horse's flesh. People often think that thick flocking will protect the horse, but this simply isn't the case. The inside of the saddle has to be well finished to prevent problems. Once Kay had removed the D-rings, which the owner had never used anyway, and re-flocked the saddle, the lumps disappeared. It's dreadful to think that lumps might have been cut out of the horse's back rather than the saddle.*

**INTELLIGENT HORSEMANSHIP RECOMMENDED ASSOCIATE JULIA SCHOLES**

3 Once you know that you can get the bit in, make sure the bridle fits loosely so it's going to be easy to put over his ears. Remember, ears prick – come forward; they don't squash down conveniently to allow bridles to be put on. Go for one ear at a time. Personally, I find if there's any difficulty it's easier and more comfortable for the horse if I do the near ear from the nearside and then go round and do the off ear from the offside.

## PROBLEMS PUTTING ON THE BRIDLE

When someone can't get the bridle on a horse, then I go over and am able to get it on, I find the difference is usually one of attitude because they are almost 'trying too hard'. I come over and act as if I'm not really that bothered. The horse may fuss around for a while and I just stay with him and the horse seems to realize I'm not there for a fight, but just to get a job done and he relaxes. If the horse has a real ear problem that we haven't had the opportunity to deal with before, I may slip the browband off, undo the headpiece, then get the bit in and do the headpiece up over the top of his neck. The most important thing is your attitude, that you don't get anxious. You may want someone to teach you the practicalities to start with, but then I think it helps for you to work with the horse privately for a while, without the feeling that anyone is rushing you or judging you. Sometimes you can get anxious because you're worried about what other people might think – remember, the most important thing is what your horse thinks.

## 'BLOWING OUT WITH THE GIRTHS'
### HOW THIS PROBLEM STARTS

This is a defence mechanism. When a poor horse has had the girths hoicked up insensitively time after time, he learns to 'blow himself out' to make his girth area as large as possible. This starts a vicious circle with the rider, who, understandably, doesn't want to risk the girths slipping, attempting to pull up the girths tighter and tighter because she knows the horse is blowing out, which gives the horse full justification to blow out more and more.

We've already talked about horses pushing against pressure unless taught otherwise. The tighter you pull the girths, the harder the horse pushes against them. I have seen racehorses come up with massive blood blisters from the jockey over-tightening the girths and it must surely have prevented many horses from giving a top performance over the years. I can't do better than to quote from Kay Humphries' excellent book *Saddle Fitting* published by J. A. Allens, where she states that leather girths, if kept soft and supple, are the most comfortable for the horse. She also says: 'Where there is elastic on one side, this is for the horse's comfort and not for your benefit! The elastic should always be done up on the offside and, when the rider is in the saddle, their girth should only be tightened on the nearside. This allows the horse to breathe. If you tighten the elastic side from on top, two things will happen; one is that it is likely that you will overtighten the girth and the second is that by stretching the elastic you will in fact pull the saddle over to that side.'

### THINGS YOU CAN DO TO HELP

To prevent a girth problem with your youngsters, do up their girths firmly but gently. I always use a breast girth when I'm starting young horses, so I know the saddle won't slip back if the girths aren't on as firmly as they should be. It tends to be a certain type of horse that saddles are most likely to slip on. They slip to the side on very round horses with no discernible backbone, and they slip back on those with a more tubular shape, known as 'herring gutted', because they have no belly to hold the girths in place. These horses are better with a breast girth and wearing a good non-slip pad for safety.

The most important thing for general riding is to get a saddle that is properly measured to fit your horse. The saddle is much less likely to slip if it is fitted in the right position. Most people put their horses saddles on too far forward. Put your hand against your horse's shoulder and find where the scapula is. The saddle must fit a finger width's behind this. If your saddle is too far forward and sitting on the shoulder, the saddle will twist from left to right across the spine as each shoulder moves. At the same time, the horse has to lift the saddle and you and stretch the girth on every stride. For most horses a well-fitting saddle and a reasonable girth pressure – firm, but so someone could still slip a hand between horse and girth comfortably when the rider is on top – should really be secure enough.

If your horse has got into the habit of blowing out as hard as he can, consider using a breast girth and/or a non-slip pad to make you feel more secure.

1 When you're ready, with the saddle in the corrrect position, gently do the girths up as much as the horse will comfortably allow from the ground and then walk him round a few steps. Repeat this process and check them again once you are on board, again not getting into a battle but just ensuring the girths are in a comfortable spot.

2 Check again before you prepare to go into a trot or faster work. This will make the situation manageable, and hopefully it will gradually start to reassure your horse that it's not necessary for him to blow himself up like a balloon every time you are preparing for a ride.

*Although I will always try to give you the guidelines that will help you and your horse, remember that anything you do to increase your horse's trust and respect at any time is going to improve your relationship and increase your chances of success.*

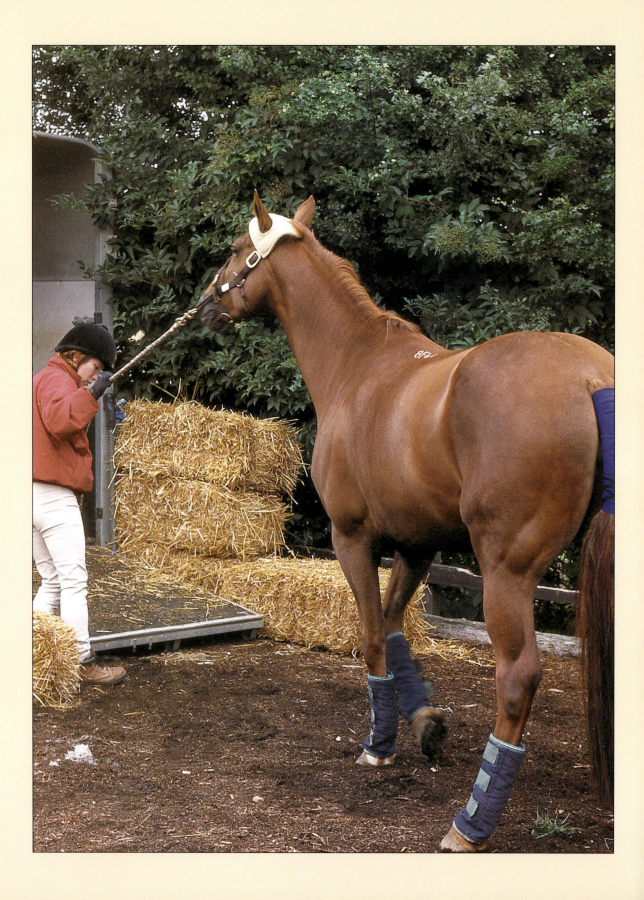

# *time to*
# TRAVEL

Horses that won't load into a horsebox or trailer are one of the major causes of misery and frustration for the horse owner. I remember a pony of mine having an aversion to loading (he didn't seem to mind the actual travelling). Not only were many hours spent in the early mornings before leaving for shows fussing around with food, coaxing and pleading, but we had to go through the whole rigmarole to get home again. It's much harder at the actual show ground because of the enormous amount of 'experts' popping out from behind every horsebox: 'Hit him with a broom, that'll move him'; 'I've got a lunge whip in the trailer, that's what he needs.' Tempting as it is to take up these offers when you've been getting nowhere for a couple of hours, let me assure you, because I've been through this scenario so many times, that as soon as they have your horse kicking out, sweating, looking behind and his head so high he couldn't possibly go in, you hear, 'Look, this isn't our problem and we've got to get off now', and your 'helpers' leave you in a mess ten times worse than when you started.

## HOW THIS PROBLEM STARTS

• The horse has never been taught to load.
• The horse has never even been taught to lead.
• The handlers have never been taught to lead and load.
• The handlers have no control of the horse, they are using entirely the wrong body language, holding the horse on far too short a lead, blocking where he's going and are not looking him in the eye.
• The trailer or horsebox is really uninviting – rickety, ramp broken, dark, smelling bad. I know of someone who couldn't get her horse in a trailer after pigs had travelled in it – he wanted it washed out before he would load, and who could blame him?
• Somebody's hit the horse from behind so he spends his whole time looking behind him now.

THE GENTLE ART
HORSES THAT WON'T LOAD ARE
A MAJOR CAUSE OF MISERY
AND FRUSTRATION.

• Somebody's hit the horse from behind, so he's thrown his head up and hit it on the horsebox and he believes going in the box is going to hurt him now.
• The horse has had a bad experience in the box with people driving it too fast.
• He's not been able to balance himself, having had to travel in a very narrow space.
• There has been an unavoidable accident while the horse was travelling in the trailer.

THINGS YOU CAN DO TO HELP

Even if your horse isn't a bad loader or a bad traveller, you still want him to have the best journey possible. Research has shown that travelling puts the horse under considerable mental and physical stress. Apart from the obvious reasons why you want him to be comfortable (he trusts you and you love him) but something you can point out to even the hardest of souls, is that the horse is going to do a much better job for you at the competition or schooling session if he isn't stressed. Even after a good journey it takes around 20 minutes for a horse's pulse rate to come back down to normal.

1 Checking the trailer. The trailer or horsebox should be checked over for complete safety and security, and it may seem obvious but make sure your trailer fits the horse. In addition, it must be clean. For long journeys a horse must be encouraged to stale, otherwise it can cause him considerable discomfort. For this he will need some straw or shavings on the floor. Shavings will soak the urine up better, but remember, it must be cleared out regularly as ammonia in a confined space can damage the respiratory system as well as being generally unpleasant. Shows and events should have areas where you can clear out your box.

I am hearing more horror stories of horses than ever before going through the floor while travelling. Very probably it is because of the use of rubber matting nowadays, which although a good idea for comfortable travelling, must be lifted regularly to air and to check what is going on underneath. Make sure too that there are no nails, screws, bolts or hooks poking out anywhere that could injure the horse. I read

GROWING PAINS

I went to load a very handsome big horse once; he was over 17hh. The preliminary work was going perfectly, I couldn't see why there would be a problem. Then the owners drove the trailer into the school for me to load him. It was a single-horse trailer suitable for a large pony. I said, 'I'm terribly sorry but I have to tell you that your trailer is too small for this horse.' They seemed quite indignant and replied, 'But we bought this trailer for him when he was 18 months old and it fitted him then!'

in a magazine once about someone who thought she'd checked out her horsebox thoroughly when suddenly she realized there was a wasps' nest hidden in a corner!

2 When they are being transported, horses are forced to lean against parts of the trailer or horsebox to balance themselves. Conveniently for us, we don't actually see the bruising this causes horses but be aware it is there.

Ask anyone who has ever travelled in the back of a trailer how insecure and uncomfortable it feels. It's actually illegal for a human being to travel in a trailer (it's considered too dangerous, which is worrying in itself). I think it should be illegal for someone not to have experienced a ride in the back before transporting horses. Trailers should not be driven at more than 30 miles an hour at any time. Horseboxes don't swing around in the same way but it's still uncomfortable for the horses if you brake suddenly. A maximum of 30 mph on country roads is advisable and 50 mph on motorways. Obviously, motorways and straighter roads are much more comfortable for horses when they are travelling, so bear this in mind when planning all your journeys. In addition:
• Look ahead, change gear early when approaching hills.
• Gear changes should be as smooth as possible. If your passengers' heads move during your gear changes, you haven't got it smooth enough yet.
• Tight corners should be taken at a crawl and sudden changes of direction should be avoided at all costs.
• If you imagine you are driving without any brakes it could help keep your mindset right for the comfort of the horse.

The box should be light and airy, with fresh air circulating, but make sure it is not draughty. I've seen great photos of mustangs travelling together in an open-topped trailer and they don't appear to be worried at all because they can see where they are going, and all the way round. You will notice that horses love to look out of a window if they can, as they are travelling along. However, thanks to student horse psychology projects with extensive video coverage of horses travelling, something has been brought to my attention that I hadn't previously considered as much as I should have before – that it's pretty frightening for horses when branches and bushes hit those windows. Of course, you can't always drive in the middle of the road but it is something to be aware of and, again, if you are driving that bit slower it's not going to take the horse by surprise so much.

3 Make sure the space is right. Studies have shown that if horses are given enough space, they will prefer to travel at a 45-degree angle and facing backwards. I've heard from people that transport several

loose horses at a time, that what horses generally seem to do is all arrange themselves at a 45-degree angle but nose to tail throughout, so some are effectively travelling forwards and some backwards.

Often when people have a 'bad traveller', which is their usual definitition of a horse that moves around a lot when travelling, their thinking goes, 'If I could just pen him in a bit tighter – that will keep him still.' I even had a lady who wrote to me saying she thought she'd solved the problem of keeping her pony still by wedging straw bales on either side of him, but that unfortunately he'd started falling on his knees. The horse would do, when you consider that the way he balances himself when travelling is to spread out his legs – you can't blame a horse for being worried; he's obviously got good cause to be. Imagine you are travelling in the back of a trailer and trying to balance yourself. Remember, the horse is not able to hold on to anything. How is it going to be easier – with your legs spread apart or your legs placed closely together? Correct. Horses tend to travel with their legs apart in a bracing position. If you have to have partitions, make sure there is a gap of at least 60cm (2ft) at the bottom of them so that the horse has the maximum room to spread his legs. Most horses travel better without partitions. Some horses travel much better completely loose, allowing them to turn around as they wish. All horses travel better if not tied tightly – they must be allowed to lower and raise their heads to balance comfortably, although you obviously need to make sure they can't get the rope caught over or under anything.

## WEIGHT DISTRIBUTION

A report in the *Veterinary Record* showed that thoroughbreds facing backwards when travelling had lower heart rates and maintained better balance. Their heart rates were also lower when loaded into trailers backwards. According to the researchers, horses 'have evolved to carry about 60 per cent of their body weight over the forelegs, and the hindquarters are poorly designed for continual weight and shifting of weight and direction.' A backward-facing horse can cope better with the swaying of the trailer, which is more pronounced at the back, and also sit in to the trailer when the driver brakes. Unfortunately, because of the 60 per cent distribution of body weight, this tends to unbalance the trailer if he's at the back and very few trailers are made to accommodate this.

4 Ensure the environment isn't cramped. Bad travellers tend to be labelled 'claustrophobic' but this may not necessarily be the case. The horse's panic may be more induced by him not being able to spread his legs. Also, do remember how horses are naturally inclined to push into pressure if they are tense or nervous. Around the flank area is a particularly sensitive spot and pressure there on a frightened horse will not only make him lean in but often down and/or kick out as well. This could be a throwback to when horses had to protect themselves from wild dogs that would go for the soft belly and flank areas and rip into the horse's

*Case study*

# THE TRAUMATIZED MARE

*I'll never forget my first solo loading job after finishing my training courses with Kelly. I remember being told on the phone that this mare was fine – you could get her into a trailer. It was only if you tried to put the ramp up quickly there was a problem because then she would fly out backwards. She sounded quite easy so I decided to go and work with her on my own and my partner, Nicole, stayed at home working with our other horses. While I was doing Join Up the owner told me a story about the partitions falling down and trapping the horse in a box on one occasion, and then there was another harrowing tale of how she had been beaten into the trailer just before the owner had bought her. That's what she meant by 'You could get her in'. I commented that she was actually a pretty badly traumatized horse, to which the owner replied, 'Oh yes, I know.' I resisted the urge to query why she hadn't mentioned any of this on the phone!*

*I didn't notice anything unusual until I was leaving the school having done some halter training, and I was leading the mare through a fairly wide door. She flew through it, nearly knocking me over. I could see just for the horse and owner's safety that some improvements had to be made there, so I ended up spending over an hour getting her to stop in any part of the doorway, and going through without rushing. I got her to the point where I could reverse her through in both directions as well as going forwards. It was such a massive phobia for her, but the owner hadn't even mentioned it. I remember I then rang home. 'How's it going?' Nicole asked, thinking I must be nearly ready to come home. 'It's going great,' I said. 'We're doing really well– I'm about to take her to the horsebox now.' I'd been there for almost three hours!*

*I was so confident that she would go in, having come so far already, but when she came round the corner and saw the box she went into a complete panic. I spent a long time working on the approach and getting her really relaxed, and when I actually got her near the trailer she went straight in after only three minutes. Within about an hour you could load her easily and put her in with the partitions up, with or without other horses, and close up the ramp without her worrying.*

*I had been so thorough with her basic training that going up the ramp was not an issue by the time we came to it. If I had not spent all that time working on going through the doorway, I'm quite sure that she would never have dealt with the partitions touching her and the ramp closing in such a short time.*

**INTELLIGENT HORSEMANSHIP RECOMMENDED ASSOCIATE ADAM GOODFELLOW**

side. The horse's immediate reaction to a sudden pressure in the flank area is to bear down in that direction and kick out – you can see how that would be a better defence from attacking dogs than running away and allowing the dogs to tear out his entrails. Watch one of the 'bad travellers' as he is going along, and you will see that when he can't balance he will lean into the partition and then, as he perceives that it is pushing into him and 'biting' him, will push back into it even more. This particularly happens on the turns, but once a horse has had a few bad experiences he's going to start falling down, kicking and panicking as soon as he feels the partitions on his sides. That's if you can get him in the box in the first place.

5 Check your horse hasn't developed a travel phobia. If a horse has developed a real phobia of travelling, to help him get over his fears and start to travel normally it may be necessary to take all the partitions out and transport him alone until you see some significant improvement. With some horses a trusted companion horse may be helpful – all horses are different. Be prepared to try different things to see what works and what doesn't. I would advise a nice full haynet for his journey. One of my students working on a horse psychology project found a marked difference for the better in the horses' heart rates when aromatherapy oils were used. She put a combination of calming oils – jasmine, frankincense and vetiver – in a base oil that was applied to the nostrils and poll area of the horse half an hour before travelling.

I would also much prefer to take a difficult traveller in a horsebox than a trailer initially, both for reasons of safety and comfort. Make sure the floor is non-slip, has plenty of straw on the surface, and that the horse is totally protected. Take him for short, straight journeys initially, driving very slowly, and drive in the middle of the road so you don't hit branches.

## LOADING YOUR HORSE

Once you have inspected your horsebox or trailer with the thoroughness of Hercule Poirot and interrogated the driver, threatening them with an unpleasant death if they drive over 30 mph, it's now time to load your horse.

The best way to get a youngster loading well is to allow him to follow his mother in when just a foal. Stud managers have noticed that the foals who have been in the horsebox with their mother when she has gone off to visit a stallion while on foaling heat (just 11 days after the birth) are very rarely concerned about loading in later life.

1 Make sure the box is light and inviting, remove any partitions inside, and load on a safe, soft surface. Consider using panels on either side of the ramp so that the right way to go is clear. Have the ramp as level as possible.

2 Anything that encourages the horse to have confidence or look forward to going in the box is a good idea. Things that can help are: a lead from an older horse, a feed waiting in the box, or manually placing one of his feet on the ramp and giving him a stroke. With a small horse

or pony who doesn't kick, linking hands behind the hindquarters and encouraging him in gently can be effective. Having done a Join Up and seen your horse gain confidence is all going to encourage him to be happy to go where you go. Give him enough time in these early stages and don't rush him. He has a right to be suspicious of this strange, moving cave you want him to go in!

## A BAD LOADER

With a really bad loader it's usually a different matter altogether. I've known people try fruitlessly for over eight hours to load a horse so that I can teach him to load at a demonstration. What I am going to describe shortly is a training method to get your horse loading perfectly – not a quick fix, but a training method that takes time. So if you haven't got the time or sufficiently safe facilities to use that method, I would suggest you either ride your horse to where you need to go or try the methods outlined earlier with infinite patience.

In an emergency, use the racehorse starting stalls method: blindfold your horse and turn him in a few circles, then get some sensible, and strong, people to help lift him in for you. However, do be very careful with this. I heard of one person who blindfolded her horse, and the horse subsequently got loose. He ran through two fences, and was heading for a brick wall, when the blindfold slipped off just in time. As I said, this may be an idea for an emergency but it is actually a good idea for horses to learn to be led in a blindfold anyway, just in case there is ever a stable fire. Remember Black Beauty? Horses' first instincts are to stand stock still in a fire, so you may have to tie your jumper over their eyes to lead them out.

If it's a remedial horse you are working on and the pair of you have not yet completed the Foundation Exercises (see pages 58-73) with the grace of Fred Astaire and Ginger Rogers – stop! Do not even think about trying to load your horse until you are doing those exercises not just perfectly, but without a moment's hesitation.

If the horse is doing the Foundation Exercises plus the appropriate Additional Yielding Exercises (see pages 74-85) perfectly and without a moment's hesitation, please read on.

• For the remedial horse a training halter during loading is an extremely useful aid (see also Training Halters, pages 37-40). They must only be used in the correct manner and on a safe surface, otherwise it would be unfair and confusing to the horse and could even be dangerous.

• Dress for success – as with the other exercises wear a hard hat, good footwear, (I also like to wear lightweight gloves), have the training halter correctly fitted, and a comfortable thick rope of at least 4.5m (15ft) in length. When loading the horse he should be wearing a poll guard and protective boots or bandages.

If you are having to load a youngster it may not be possible for him to wear boots but with an older horse part of your pre-schooling should be to introduce him to wearing boots and being able to walk in them without looking like he's taking the first steps on the moon. The schooling must be done on a safe surface in an enclosed area. Now we are going to run through those Foundation Exercises again, but within just two or three metres of the horsebox or trailer so we are gradually desensitizing the horse to its presence, at the same time as we're moving the horse around. You do those perfectly, of course, and now let's ask the horse for a movement towards the horsebox. Back away from him at a slight angle and apply light pressure on the rope – you are not pulling, just starting to ask. You can gradually build the pressure up and if he's more difficult than you thought, then make the angle more acute so he has to move because you've unbalanced him. Reward the slightest movement by releasing the pressure instantly, allow him a moment to think and then give him a lovely rub.

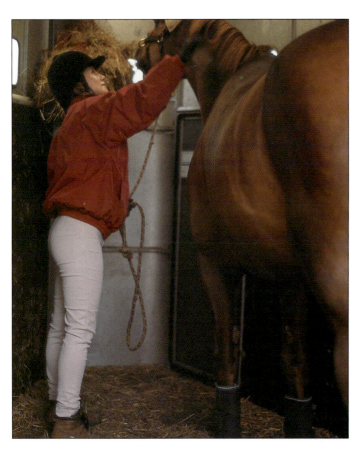

### REWARD HIM FOR EVEN THINKING THE RIGHT WAY

There's the saying 'A good horseman can hear a horse talk, a great horseman can hear a horse whisper'. I had a delightful Irish student, now an IH Recommended Associate, Padraic Foy, who put in his exam: 'A good horseman can hear a horse whisper but a great horseman can hear a horse think.' I thought that was funny at the time but the more I think about it the more I think maybe he's the one who got it right. It's no easy thing, hearing a horse think, but here are some pointers that might help. Reward the horse with release of pressure and a general relaxation if he even just so much as to focuses in the right direction. Watch his chest as you're asking him forward; if he just moves his chest forward a little again, release the pressure. Work on pressure/release with a human friend. Shut your eyes, or get blindfolded if you're the sort of person that cheats, and ask your friend to hold one end of your rope. You are to tell them the second you feel them

**A REWARDING SITUATION** BE SURE YOUR HORSE GETS PRAISED FOR HAVING DONE THE RIGHT THING.

move and instantly put your hand down, into the 'release' position. When you're getting really good you can ask your friend to move the rope to either side or slightly up or slightly down and you tell her which way she's moving it. Having your eyes closed will increase your sensitivity and you need to bring the experience of it into your work with loading the horse. Remember, this sensitivity and the use of pressure and release apply throughout our horsemanship.

### THE HORSE 'MORSE CODE'
This is a completely brilliant expression that was coined by horseman David Dodswell and is now the title of a book. David has lectured to my students and just the title alone, *The Horse Morse Code*, reminds us that we shouldn't be attempting to pull and push our horses around. Instead, we are using a series of cues and are actually teaching them a series of signals that they learn to pck up on. Next time your horse is pawing the ground in frustration, make sure it's not SOS he's spelling out.

### OTHER EXERCISES BEFORE GOING TO THE HORSEBOX
You know we want to set our horses up for success. This is what I want to do for you as well. Nothing works like success! We have established a strong foundation and now I want you to set up a series of goals for you and your horse.
• The first exercise could be to walk over a narrow piece of tarpaulin on the ground. There may be resistance but you can work through this; it is a good idea to get someone to evaluate your body language and timing. All the time you are creating a greater bond of trust and understanding and you are both growing in confidence.
• Get your horse to go over a fully laid-out tarpaulin.
• Walk him over wooden bridges.
• Get him to go in between straw bales.
• Walk him under a tarpaulin.
  If you feel you are going to have resistance, work through these methods first and get your horse thoroughly habituated to them before risking loading him into the horsebox.

### MORE PRESSURE AND RELEASE TIPS
It's all about good communication. If you keep talking all the time, the other person may want to say something, something really positive, but how can they if they can't get a word in? They need a space in order to give their message. With people, good manners encourage you to pause a moment to see what the other person has to say. Some people, of course, will just carry on talking, never giving a thought to what the other person might want to say. We need to train ourselves to hear what a horse is thinking. If given the slightest indication of a forward movement, we should release the pressure totally and allow him some time. If he's so much as thinking about moving forwards, relax and give him as much time as he needs. The horse actually often makes the forward move not on the pressure, but on the release.

## THERE'S NOTHING LIKE THE REAL THING

You are now at the horsebox or trailer. You've not only done the Foundation Exercises, some Additional Yielding Exercises (see pages 58-73 and 74-85) and some tarpaulin and bridge work, but you've even been doing these things close to the horsebox so the horse's pulse rate is no longer going up any more every time he gets near the box. So now you can back your horse up a few strides, ask him forward a few strides (don't forget to give lots of reward) and all the while get closer to the box until you are standing on the ramp and you are asking the horse to step on to the ramp.

1 Make sure you are never standing directly in front of him, but always at an angle to one side or another, and work with the pressure and release, as described above. Don't immediately try and hurry the horse on; take some time to reward him for just having a foot on the ramp. Then you may ask him to take a step backwards and then ask for that foot on the ramp again. Reward him as you work and use your judgement as to whether it is appropriate to ask for yet one more step up the ramp.

2 I have found it effective to sometimes crouch down slightly on a steep ramp – horses are less comfortable when you are towering over them. Also it's not a bad idea to lean down slightly the very first time your horse comes near the ramp to encourage him to put his head down and have a look at it. Remember, he can't see where he's putting his feet if his head is held high.

3 Letting him look a couple of times is sufficient; after that you want him to put his trust in you and come forward even if he is still slightly unsure. With your horse on the ramp, renew the tension lightly until you receive the next forward motion, and reward him again.

4 Once you have achieved the goal of getting your horse in the horsebox, your work is by no means finished. Consider that you have achieved half your goal. You should now take the time to lead your horse up and down the ramp at least six times until you feel he is totally comfortable. Put a haynet in the horsebox so he even starts to look forward to going in.

5 Once he is relaxed in the box, you also need to check that you can move him one step at a time, forwards and backwards. It's no good if you take one step back and he rushes out. How are you ever going to do up the ramp? You need to aim to be able to control each foot smoothly and easily.

## WHAT TO DO IF IT'S NOT WORKING
### 'MY HORSE JUST JUMPS OFF THE SIDE OF THE RAMP'

He should be following your line and if he starts to veer off at any stage you need to direct him back on course straight away. You could consider using panels to fence in the sides of the ramp to close off the horse's options and make it easier for him to do the right thing. This is a good approach for youngsters as well. I will often use panels from a round pen, but if these aren't available just use your imagination – park the trailer by a wall or fence, or use an old gate or door to enclose the other side. Remember always to think through any safety issues.

### 'MY HORSE RUSHES OUT BACKWARDS'

If he does go to rush out backwards, you don't want to hold him tightly and risk him throwing his head up and maybe even hitting it on the roof of the horsebox, so initially let him go the few steps necessary so that his head is clear of the roof, then take a firm hold and 'catch' him. When he stops, ask tactfully for a step forward again. If this gets particularly difficult with a big, strong horse, you can think about using panels along the ramp and then enclosing the horse from behind as well. If you use a front-loading trailer, this discourages this habit.

### 'I CAN'T GET MY HORSE OUT OF THE TRAILER'

This was a real phone call I received. It shows why you need to do all those Foundation Exercises, including the backing up, before you start loading! You have to reverse the process, in a manner of speaking; do the 'one step at a time' schooling while in the trailer to get him out. Don't panic. He will come out eventually. He just needs a bit of time.

### 'MY HORSE PLANTS HIMSELF AND WON'T COME FORWARD'

It may be that you need to be using a slightly stronger training halter. If you keep pressure on a horse for, say, over 30 seconds, and he's really leaning and you see his eyes starting to glaze, this means endorphins are beginning to be released due to the pressure on the spot behind the ears. If you just hold, the reaction you get is likely to be dramatic – a half rear and a run backwards. It's best to avoid a horse getting like this by shifting your position from side to side, keeping the tension fluid so you don't encourage the horse to lean. Don't forget to release at the slightest forward movement. For a horse like this it may be better not to put any pressure on his head but just encourage him in with panels all round. Keep the concept in mind of making it uncomfortable when he's doing what you don't want him to do (but comfortable when he's doing what you do want him to do). It's better to give him a little aggravation by moving his feet rather than letting him settle and stand still, so move him in whatever way you can. Keep backing up and getting him to go forward if that'll keep him moving, or keep circling him at the bottom of the ramp, then ask for a step on to it. Let him know his options – constant circling or going in the horsebox, where everything will be peaceful and tranquil.

### 'I DON'T WANT TO/CAN'T USE A TRAINING HALTER ON MY HORSE'

You have the options already mentioned – food, lead horse, panels behind to encourage him. In addition, as described above, giving the horse the 'circling option' can work very well.

### 'MY HORSE PUTS HIS HEAD SO HIGH I THINK HE'S GOING TO HIT HIMSELF'

This horse is a definite candidate for both a poll guard and for practising going under a tarpaulin before attempting to lead him under the horsebox roof. What you will learn if you practise taking your horse under the tarpaulin is that he will deliberately hold his head high to start with, as if to say, 'I can't possibly do this. I'm far too big, anyone can see that.' However, if you keep gently persisting, he'll gradually drop his head. If he does throw his head up into the tarpaulin, it's not going to harm him and you can keep practising further until he relaxes.

### 'I GET HIS FRONT FEET IN BUT HE WON'T PUT HIS BACK FEET IN'

I've found this on some occasions, particularly with very tall horses. I've suspected it has something to do with their brains being a long way from their feet. This happens with youngsters because they haven't worked out exactly how their back legs/feet work. See Sensitivity to Picking up Feet and Leg Handling (pages 160-5) and do extra work on the legs. If he's happy having his back legs handled, try just picking up one leg and placing it on the ramp, then telling him how clever he is.

### 'MY HORSE TRIES TO RUN BACK AS SOON AS YOU GO TO PUT THE RAMP UP'

You need to have fingertip control once the horse is in the horsebox, and be able to place each foot exactly where you want it. Get him so focused on you that he's not thinking about the ramp. If he does run backwards immediately, ask him straight back in again. Don't make a big deal of anything. If you have to ask him in and out one hundred times – so what? Just think of it as spending quality time with your horse. He'll soon understand running out is not worth the effort. Make sure that the people putting up the ramp do so slowly, and check that the ramp can close quietly. This might be a good time to oil the hinges! Also, make sure that they stand to one side, and that they know not to try to hold the ramp up against the weight of the horse. If the horse does charge out, and they let go of the ramp, the ramp might not appreciate it, but the chances of injury to horse or humans is much reduced. Obviously, at this stage, you won't have the option of putting up the bracing straps of a trailer, as the partitions are not in place. Make sure when you're ready to go for this option that the horse is used to the feel of objects on his legs – say the leg straps of a rug, or long lines. If you put up the bracing straps and the horse tries to run out backwards, he could end up sitting on them and panicking, and is quite likely to rear, so really make sure the horse is happy with the ramp going up first.

## 'MY HORSE SEEMS GENUINELY FRIGHTENED OF THE HORSEBOX/TRAILER'

Horses don't lie. We may misread what they're saying, i.e. a horse saying, 'I'm full of the joys of spring today so I'm going to hop about and lark around a bit' may be interpreted by someone as, 'pretending to be frightened'. But if you think your horse looks genuinely frightened of the trailer, then you are more than likely right – and he has every right to be – so take time to introduce it into his life.

If you have your horse turned out, park the trailer or horsebox near the water trough and place any feeds and hay on the ramp. As his confidence grows you can move the feeds progressively further into the horsebox. We did this with a horse called Fergus last summer. His owners had been trying to load him for two years and hadn't succeeded. The facilities weren't safe or suitable for using a training halter so at about 6pm we turned him out in a 15m (50ft) round pen with the trailer pointing into the pen and hay going from the ramp to right inside the trailer. Fergus was happily eating the hay on the ramp during the evening as we left him. A friend

### OLLIE THE ORPHAN

I once had to deal with a totally unhandled foal by the name of Ollie who had been orphaned on the Welsh hillside and turned up lost and lonely in the garden of Chris and Veronica Flynn. The Flynn family immediately adopted him but were a little concerned how to progress and rang me about bringing their little 'wild boy' to a demonstration I was giving in Bridgend, Wales. 'But if he's that wild is it going to be a problem getting him to the demonstration?' I asked. 'Not at all!' they said. 'We've made Ollie a shelter out of our trailer in the garden and he's fed his hay in there. He loves his trailer!' What a brilliant idea!

sleeping in a caravan nearby actually heard his feet starting to go up the ramp as the hay was fully eaten by 11.50pm. Once the actual fear and suspicion had been overcome, it was a much easier and safer procedure to load him the next day.

## 'I STILL CAN'T LOAD MY HORSE' OR 'I'M STILL WORRIED'

Find something your horse can do successfully. Let him do it and tell him how good he is. Alternatively, call the Intelligent Horsemanship Association (see page 222) and ask them to send someone out to help you.

PART 3

*deepening*
YOUR
KNOWLEDGE

# *behaviourism* FOR BEGINNERS

We probably all know someone who can 'talk well'. We may even be a little in awe of them when they are telling us of their horse's 'tonic immobility'. 'It's awful,' they say, 'and the various sequelae progress insidiously to ensure further recumbency through physical factors.' You nod sympathetically as they go on to tell us about their other horse's 'persistent anomalous oral-ingestive behaviour'. 'Oh dear,' you say, desperately trying to look intelligent.

It's not rare to find, though, when you get to see these people actually near a horse, that they are totally incompetent. 'Hmmm,' you think. 'They should stick to talking.' It's quite clearly the case that knowing all the right words does not necessarily make you a good horseperson. However, to be fair, it doesn't necessarily make you a bad one either.

I'm not alone in not believing that behaviourism has all the answers. Vicki Hearne in her book *Adam's Task – Calling Animals by Name* says that, in her experience, 'in obedience and riding classes, people with training in the behavioural sciences hadn't much chance of succeeding with their animals'. What, I believe, she means is that people with rigid ideas of how animals 'should' react but who lack any sort of flair or feeling for the animal are at a considerable disadvantage. Having said that, so long as we keep working on our 'feeling and flair', sometimes having a framework of knowledge to build our work around can be an advantage. It can give us a structure to help think through various challenges. Just so long as you don't make that framework too narrow and those 'words' a block to communicating with less-informed people or robbing you of your imagination.

## A BRIEF HISTORY OF BEHAVIOURISM

Behaviourism was first introduced by John B. Watson in the early 1900s. Watson argued that if psychology were to be a science then its data must be observable and measurable. It was found that a great deal of learning is associative, meaning that certain actions follow other

DESENSITIZING

TAKE TIME TO GET YOUR HORSE

USED TO DIFFERENT THINGS.

actions. Traditionally, there are two kinds of associative learning that have been of interest: classical conditioning and operant conditioning.

In classical conditioning, the subject learns that one event follows another. The most famous experiment illustrating this was that of Ivan Pavlov and his dogs. Pavlov, a Russian physiologist, noticed that his dogs salivated at the sight of a food dish. He experimented with turning on a light just before giving the dogs the meat. The dogs soon salivated as the light was turned on because they associated the light with the food.

In operant conditioning, the subject learns that a response made will be followed by a particular consequence. Thorndike and B. F. Skinner were the main players in this field. They found that an organism learns that a response it makes will be followed by a particular consequence. Thorndike's original experiment was to observe the behaviour of cats that were confined in a cage. To get out they had to lift a simple latch. Initially their behaviour consisted of random clawing and scratching until they opened the mechanism by chance. When the cat was returned to the cage it took less time to release itself, by eliminating previous unsuccessful responses, but the learning was gradual. This was termed 'trial and error' learning. This principle Thorndike formulated into his Law of Effect, in other words that successful behaviour will be repeated – successful in the sense that the subject gets the desired result or reward for his actions.

In 1938, B. F. Skinner published his book *The Behaviour of Organisms*, in which he described the results of reinforcement experiments on rats in which lever pressing was learned in order to obtain food and water, and, on these findings, outlined the basic principles of operant behaviour. This pioneering work gradually influenced other experimental psychologists to begin studying the effects of reinforcement on the behaviour of rats and other animals.

In 1953, Skinner published his book *Science and Human Behaviour*, in which he offered his interpretation of how the basic behavioural principles influence the actions of people in all kinds of everyday situations. During the 1950s there were many experiments that demonstrated that the consequences of actions influence human and animal behaviour in predictable ways. (Common sense really.)

### DEFINITIONS OF BEHAVIOURIST TERMS
Be aware that behaviourists and scientists are an argumentative bunch and argue about precise meanings of many terms. However, the following are generally understood to be the correct definitions.

### POSITIVE REINFORCEMENT
A positive reinforcement is something pleasant that takes place at the time of the good behaviour which will reinforce (i.e. strengthen) that

behaviour. Connected with this are 'primary' or 'conditioned' reinforcers (see pages 204-6).

## THE 'LOVELY HEAD RUB'

This is an action that can really strengthen your bond with your horse. You stand to the front of your horse, slightly to one side, and move one hand smoothly up to gently rub your fingers in circular motions in the area between his eyes. Let your horse relax and feel really comfortable with the experience. Take your time and enjoy the moment yourself. For many years horsemen, particularly those most likely to be known as 'whisperers', have used this particular gesture. Why would this movement have any more effect on a horse than any other? Some people believe it's significant that it's an area the horse can't see or touch himself, although that could apply to other areas of the horse as well. Many of us know the joys of a facial and perhaps the feel of massaging movements close to the brain are particularly pleasant and soothing. It is said the action can release endorphins to the brain.

People who practise the massage technique Shiatsu talk about the area called the 'third eye' being located one-third of the way up the centre line of the forehead. Pamela Hannay, a leading authority on Shiatsu for horses, states, 'It's an important area because it's the focal point of the "inner eye", the spirit. It's said that this area can sense energy, and is the gate through which to calm the mind and reach intuitive knowledge.' Whichever explanation you favour, and it may be a combination of all three, if you take the time to experience it with your horse, you will often be aware of a feeling of peace coming over both of you.

This is not something you can achieve instantly with a horse. It may be several days before an anxious horse will accept you in this area and even longer before he actually stands still and focuses on the experience. Achieving that alone is a great step forward.

A LOVELY RUB
A LOVELY RUB CAN INCREASE YOUR MUTUAL BOND.

In our busy lives we're often rushing around so much that we miss the important things. People sometimes ask me if telepathy exists between horses and humans. Can we transfer thoughts between each other? Can we really understand what the other is thinking? All I can answer is, that just supposing it did exist, it is not going to be possible

*Case study*

# HORSE/HUMAN TELEPATHY

*There are good and bad practitioners of everything. We are even aware nowadays that there are bad doctors, bad priests, even bad mothers. We are probably all aware that there can be phoney and dishonest 'psychics' about. This is indisputable. A few years ago I went to see a horse who wouldn't load in the horsebox. I said to the lady owner that there would be no charge for my services if she didn't mind me bringing some students along to watch how I worked. I went to see the horse, a lovely big animal. Lovely lady owner too. She told me how a quite well-known 'horse psychic' had already been to see him and she had 'told her' that the horse didn't like the owner's husband and that he was worried about what was going on. 'Mind you,' said the owner, 'that didn't help him go into the horsebox!'*

*I felt rather sorry that the lady believed all this; I knew I could get the horse in the horsebox using clear, consistent methods as outlined in Time to Travel (see pages 182-95). Sure enough, I worked with the horse and got him going into the horsebox at the end. But, sure enough, there were other dynamics at work. The lady's husband came out and was charming and brought out lemonade for me and my students, and I watched the interaction between the husband and wife, just generally, as you do. After the horse was going up and down the ramp really easily, I handed him over to the lady and suggested she try loading him herself. The horse started to run round her in circles and get anxious, which is a really unusual thing to happen. The husband immediately said, 'There you are, you see, it's all your fault', which of course only served to make her (and the horse) even more anxious. She did take the horse up into the horsebox a couple of times, and gradually became more relaxed so that she was able to load him for a journey she wanted to do a couple of days later, but it was a very strange afternoon. I thought through it a lot on the way home and I've thought about it more and more since. I've always been able to pick up quite strong feelings of emotion from horses (sadness, emptiness, fear, lack of confidence, as well as the positive emotions); however, I always found specific messages hard to take seriously. After that day, though, I really think the horse psychic was very close to the truth. At the very least, the horse was aware there was an uneasy atmosphere between the couple and it was making him anxious. If they were unhappy, he could have deduced, like a dog might, and even the way a very young child can, 'Is it all my fault they're unhappy?' I think it's important that we appreciate a horse is capable of these emotions (some people even imagine their children are blind to these things). I know of some outstanding results from horse healers, and now with any horse psychic I would certainly listen respectfully to what they have to say and see if it matches what I'm hearing from the horse – it's certainly very interesting.*

while we are rushing around with our heads in a whirl, saying, 'Oh, my goodness, I've got this deadline I'm going to miss and 50 emails to answer and I haven't even done the shopping yet!' It can only really happen if we take a little time and give it some thought. Sometimes people say how the time they spend with their horse is wonderful because it releases so much of their stress. I suggest we try to get rid of that stress before it gets to our horses. We know horses pick up our tension and emotions, so let's spare them this. Relax with some music or maybe do a ten-minute meditation before you go out to your horse so he doesn't have to pick up all that negative energy. Then spend the first minutes giving your horse the lovely head rub, have a relaxing sigh, and appreciate the time you are spending with this gorgeous animal and let him know he's special enough to be the focus of your attention.

## NEGATIVE REINFORCEMENT

Negative reinforcement means reinforcing (strengthening) a response by taking away an unpleasant stimulus. This is often confused with punishment and because the word 'negative' is included it suggests it must be something unpleasant or cruel. Although it's possible that this may be the case, it certainly doesn't have to be. Negative reinforcement is one of the most common ways we work with our horses and it is the basis of the 'pressure and release' work and many of the aids we give. For instance, if we put a little pressure on the reins, the horse responds in the way we desire, so we instantly release the pressure as a reward to the horse and to show him he has given the correct response.

## PUNISHMENT

This is an aversion stimulus that takes place after an event that weakens the required action or response made. Punishment generally involves pain. One of the downsides of using pain with animals or humans is that it tends to cause fear, which can often be a block to learning – 'adrenaline up; learning down'. Humans in particular, are likely to feel resentment but this is not exclusive to them; horses have been frequently known to 'get people back' as well. Punishment can't teach new behaviour, only what to avoid. It will never produce impeccable behaviour; horses and people will only work to the level required to avoid the punishment. It can only teach what to avoid or not to do. As with everything, correct timing makes an enormous difference and there is a vast potential for mistakes. If a horse stops at a jump, the rider then pushes herself up in the saddle while the horse is turning round and starts to hit him, it may only serve to make the horse run away from the jumps a great deal quicker in the future.

I would love to say that punishment never works for horses. Sadly I can't. Fear is a motivation for both horses and people. I have seen very strong, very tough people have great success in competition with horses. If those horses went to 'weaker' people they would refuse to perform because they were only ever doing it under sufferance.

Any moment of inattention from his regular rider would result in the horse taking advantage of the moment. I've heard of people getting a horse to stand still after kicking it in the stomach or whipping the horse into the horsebox. I have also heard of these same people being badly injured or even killed after a horse suddenly kicked them for 'no reason at all'. Of course, it's not unknown for people to kill either, when they've just been pushed too far and had enough of bullying behaviour.

The majority of horses that come to me with behavioural problems have already had those tactics tried on them and they've only succeeded in making the horse a great deal worse. If you are not very strong and hard, I suggest the tough route is never going to work for you. The only way you are going to have fun and competition success (if that is what you want) is to get horses to want to perform for you and to enjoy their work. If you are very strong, you have a more difficult decision. More and more people who can make the decision to try and do everything by force (including those who have tried that route in the past), have thought it through, and found a better, more satisfying way forward.

Competition is not for everyone, but I am glad I have had experience of it, and even some success, just so I can stand and say with an ever-growing band of people, 'There! You can do this as a celebration of the horse – rather than at his expense'. The choice is yours.

## PRIMARY REINFORCER

This satisfies basic drives, things that the horse naturally appreciates – so it is helpful here to think of a horse in the wild. What would he naturally like? A pat? No! A 'Good boy!'? Meaningless! Would he appreciate food? Yes! Companionship? Now you're getting the idea! And another thing he would definitely appreciate is his freedom or 'space'. This is why, if you are working with an untouched horse, the best way for you to reward him for letting you come a little closer into his comfort zone, is to immediately move away. This is the best reward you can give him. It also allows it to sink in that you are obviously not a predator and therefore a danger, because if you were, you would kill him as soon as you got close enough. Giving some 'space' works for both nerv-

### A CHILDREN'S STORY OF THE VALUE OF FREEDOM

Isn't it funny the things you can remember from being a child? I particularly remember a little book I had about a very handsome, vain young horse who lived in a herd. He was always telling the other horses how he was better than any of them. One day the king drove past and saw this handsome young horse and said if he would pull his carriage for ten years he would give him 'a prize worth more than all the money in my kingdom'. So off went the handsome young horse and worked for all he was worth every hour of every day in all weathers to win this great prize. When the ten years was up the poor old horse was tired and worn and on his last legs. The king took him back to the herd where the other horses were and said, 'Now I am going to give you the prize worth more than all the money in my kingdom – your freedom!'
The horse looked at the king and looked at the herd and the green, green fields. He didn't argue with the king. He knew he was right. He just cantered away joyfully into the distance.

ous horses and people, who, on the whole, dislike being 'too pressured' by sales people or in relationships. No one wants to feel forced into things; they want to be an active part of the process. Take a step back. You'll often find your horse taking a step towards you then.

## CONDITIONED (OR SECONDARY) REINFORCER

This is something that you learn to appreciate because it is associated with the arrival of a reinforcement. Soon it can become a reinforcement in itself. For example, in dolphin training, because the trainers can't always get the fish to the dolphin at exactly the right moment, they pair the sound of a whistle with the giving of reinforcements so they can 'reward' the dolphin with the whistle sound at the height of his jump. Whistles are great for this work because they can be heard under water. With horses a special touch or a 'Good!' are usually the most practical measures. (See also The Use of your Voice in Training, pages 49-54). In dog training, 'clickers' have become very popular. A clicker is a little box-shaped piece of equipment that fits in your hand easily. When it is pushed down it makes a 'click' sound (see page 48).

We've talked about what a wild horse naturally appreciates. A wild horse won't even appreciate a stroke when he first meets a human being. As trust builds, though, if you stroke him a couple of times and then reward him by walking away, after a while he may reconsider your presence. You've never hurt him and you seem to be the source of his food and water. You are a source of companionship as well, and after a while you go in and stroke him and just scratch that itchy bit at the withers like another horse would and: 'Hey! What do you know? It actually feels quite good!' In the best-case scenarios our horses actually start to look at us as 'generalized positive reinforcers' (make sure you drop that one in at your next social evening); in other words he sees you as the source of all good things. When a horse actually likes you, it will matter to him if you are pleased with him or not. He'll learn that 'Good boy!' means you're pleased, and strokes and pats mean the same. In some Western horsemanship training they use only negative reinforcement as a reward, claiming this is the horse's first 'language' (I'm not arguing) but, furthermore, that 'praise should only be used for kids and employees'. I disagree; they're missing out, in my opinion, on a really beneficial additional form of communication with horses (as well as partners and lovers).

It is essential with horses that a bond is established first so that the horse actually cares whether he has pleased you or not. You know how it is when a person you can't stand comes up and says, 'Oh, well done! That was so good' ('for you' implied). It just makes you want to cringe. It would be very different if a friend or someone we respected said it. Once you have the bond with a horse it is remarkable the results you can get from patting and stroking, and it can further build on the bond of trust, making it even stronger.

## STIMULUS

Anything that causes some kind of behavioural response in a horse is called a stimulus.

### GIVING REWARD

When I was working with horses in Belgium in 1999, I was watched by some charming people from a Natural Horsemanship School. ( I must admit to be a little bemused by its name, 'The Robert Redford School of Horse Whispering' – however, that's really irrelevant.) They were very positive about my work but just had a couple of questions. 'Why did I wear a hard hat while I was working?' (they were satisfied with my considered answer – I didn't just say I generally work better conscious) and 'Why did I pat my horses?' I knew where this question was 'coming from' since natural horsemanship generally states that you 'shouldn't pat your horse because horses don't pat each other'. (I've never been totally comfortable with this train of thought since horses don't put saddles on each other and ride each other about either, but I don't wish to be pedantic.) My answer in this case to the RRSHW was to explain that when I am working with young and nervous horses I like to introduce patting gently into the procedure as early as appropriate. I want to feel quite sure that the horse is happy with the sensation and with my hands moving all around him. If I'm having to walk around him as if on egg shells, I certainly wouldn't feel confident enough to put a rider up or get on myself. In the early stages of dealing with horses I find that they certainly prefer to be stroked rather than patted and perhaps later on, too, although there are massage strokes that incorporate patting which the horses seem to find pleasant. Study your horse to let him tell you what he likes best and the most important thing is creating a bond with your horse so that he wants to please you. Then he will be happy to receive patting, strokes, voice praise, whatever you care to offer him. If you are just a source of mistrust, the only rewards are going to be negative reinforcements, i.e. letting him rest and leaving him alone.

### FADING THE STIMULUS

The first time your niece comes in the house wearing dirty boots you may shout, 'Hey, out!' at her. Soon, as she starts to understand the rules, you only have to look at her feet and she immediately withdraws out of the house to take them off. You have successfully faded the stimulus. With horses you don't want to spend your time shoving and pulling on them; you fade the stimulus so they are responsive to your smallest cues. To be fair on the horse, you have to do your best to ensure that everyone else who handles them uses the same light cues.

### SHAPING

This is reinforcing all responses in 'successive approximations' that come closer to the required goal. Have you ever wondered how they teach dolphins to jump out of the water? One way is to start rewarding the dolphin with fish (primary reinforcer) any time he happens to stick his nose out of the water and also linking the fish with a whistle blow (conditioned reinforcer). Gradually, they ask the dolphin for a little more effort, then a little more, until he's eventually leaping right out of the water at the blow of the whistle. This is a very important consider-

*Case study*

# PRAISING A HORSE

*In my jockey days, (I rode on the flat and over jumps), I was given an ex-flat racehorse who I was told 'would not jump'. Riding out six days a week, I liked, on my day off – you've guessed it – to go out riding. I took Top of the Table, who I called Toppo, up the gallops to the faggots (tiny bundle of twigs in a line, just in case you weren't sure), and with some effort and with no pressure from anyone else being around, he managed to trample over them. For this I made out he'd just won the Grand National – loads of praise and enthusiastic patting and stroking. Then we made our wavery way towards them and trampled back over them on the way home as well. 'You're fantastic!' I told him. Although praise isn't the horse's first language, he can learn to enjoy these rewards, especially if you can couple them with the greatest reward of all – release of pressure. If you jump off your horse just after he has completed some difficult movement, loosen the girths and give him a lovely rub, it will very likely log into his brain: 'This is a good move to make!' I did the same thing again a couple of times and jumped off and led him home. This little ritual went on for five Sundays, improving a little more every time, until he was popping over smaller-sized hurdles nicely and it was thought time to enter him for a race, 'just to see what happens'. Nobody asked how this horse had suddenly started jumping just from being taken on Sunday hacks. I never discussed my 'schooling techniques' because I felt I'd be put down for being 'too soft' (it was hard enough as it was getting rides in races as a lady jockey). Top of the Table went out and won his first race. As sometimes happens in racing, rather than everyone going into rapturous excitement about this surprise success, they all stood in dumbfounded horror. Disaster! Nobody had bet on him and won money. Well, I had told them he was jumping well. Can't blame me and Toppo if people just won't listen.*

ation in our training of horses. How many times have you seen people battling with picking up a horse's foot when they haven't even trained the horse to stand still or to be happy with having their legs touched all over? One step at a time as they say at Alcoholics Anonymous (so I've heard). When you are looking for the end result you would like to achieve, break down what you have to accomplish into manageable steps and get each one right before moving on to the next. I find 'breaking things down into manageable chunks' very helpful in all problem solving. Next time you are faced with a challenge write it down and analyse it. Once it's there in black and white, you will often find it's made up of several separate components and manageable if you take a breath and work through one step at a time. Whatever happens, finish on a high note when training with something the horse can do well.

## SCHEDULES OF REINFORCEMENT

This means how often you use positive reinforcements or rewards. The options are continuous, fixed and variable. In the early stages of working with a horse or, for instance, potty training your child, you are going to reward continuously, take every opportunity to demonstrate your pleasure and show they've done the right thing. This doesn't continue indefinitely (in the case of the child, for instance, once they've started university it would be impractical). After a while, once you are sure the horse clearly understands your requests, you can space the rewards out a little more. So, for instance, he starts to jumps three or four jumps at a time before you tell him he's a great champion and he's sure to win at *The Horse of the Year Show*.

I think the closest I've got to using fixed rewards with horses is after every showjumping round or at the end of a race. I've never thought about rewarding after every third jump or every two furlongs. Fixed rewards are very common for most people, though. Some people receive their reward of money (incidentally money is a conditioned reinforcer, having no intrinsic value of itself but being associated with good things) at the end of every working day, at the end of the week or the end of the month.

For writers the rewards are variable (very) and this is the same with a lot of training as time moves on. While, I believe, we should not be stingy with our rewards, it's interesting how, after time, the variable form is the most addictive. It explains how people get addicted to gambling. There are slot machines around where you can put money in, and chocolate or other goodies are virtually guaranteed to come out. But thousands of people sit in Las Vegas preferring to put money in a machine where they are never quite sure if there will be any returns at all but they keep thinking the next pull is going to be 'the big one', the one that's going to pay off.

In love relationships as well, people will often find the nice, reliable person 'boring' and become addicted to the person who, though appearing to be nice initially, then starts to treat them badly. It's because 'they can be so nice sometimes' that the lover stays hooked, waiting for those less and less frequent payoffs. I'm not suggesting we should practise using these techniques to enable us to apply them with malicious intent on others, just that we should be aware of them in case we unwittingly ever find ourselves being drawn in by them.

You may wonder how you could use variable reinforcement without realizing it. Let's think about the cat that 'miaows' for his food. You refuse to feed him, absolutely refuse; it's not his feeding time and you are not going to feed him. After a while, you can't stand the noise any longer, so you give him a feed. What have you taught the cat? The value of persistence. He knows now if he just keeps going on long enough, he gets the reward. See also Scraping Doors and Floors – Everything (pages 142–4). The best way to effect a cure will probably be the ideas outlined opposite: extinction and rewarding the abscence.

## EXTINCTION

This is stopping reinforcements and letting the behavioural pattern die out. If you can stand the noise of the cat miaowing or the horse scraping and not relent, they will give up eventually. You can then try:

## REWARDING THE ABSENCE

Give the horse a reward for not doing the undesirable behaviour.

## BEHAVIOUR CHAINING

This term is the linking of several responses for reward. With behaviour chaining you generally start at the end; when the subject is finding that action easy, you then work on the actions that lead up to the grand finale. You could say it's similar to but the opposite of 'shaping'. For example, I'm not a dog trainer but having acquired the world's brightest dog, by the name of Willoughby, from a Canine Defence League home, I felt obliged to let him have a party piece to show off his talents to any guest that ever visited our home. When he was doing various attention-seeking activities around the stable yard, such as walking around with my Dandy Brush in his mouth, I would say 'fetch' as he came towards me, then give him a big hug for giving it to me. Having established 'fetch', we later got to door opening and bewildered visitors were always kept outside when they arrived and asked if they had any preference for which newspaper they would like out of a choice of two. Willoughby would be watching them in a wildly excited state. I would then say, 'Fetch the *Racing Post* Willoughby', and he would bound off, open the door with his paw and bring back the correct paper. Incidentally, I never used food in this process. I think it would have just been a distraction in this case – there are those around who are just natural-born performers. (I'm afraid how Willougby always knew the right newspaper to choose has to remain forever a secret.)

## DESENSITIZATION AND HABITUATION

These terms mean 'repeating a stimulus until there is no longer a response'. An equally adequate description would be 'getting horses used to it'. Sometimes I talk to people about 'boredom' training to try and clearly illustrate what we are trying to do. These two methods have great value in working with horses, causing them to be happier and safer. Some behaviourists use these two terms interchangeably, while others separate them with desensitization referring to a more sensory experience and habituation a more general experience. We may desensitize a horse to plastic sheets by starting off stroking him with small plastic bags until he is totally relaxed about them. We can then build up to slightly bigger bags and work with those. All the time we would be working to slightly stretch the horse's comfort zone but never to actually frighten or upset him. We continue with the occasional yawn and, 'Oh, my goodness, isn't this boring' until the horse is agreeing. We can finish the session there for the day or gradually introduce a bigger bag or more challenging things so long as there is sufficient time to continue until the total relaxation point has been reached, if, say, the horse did get a little anxious initially.

To give an example of habituation let us consider a pony that is frightened of pigs. We have looked at how you break down problems in 'One Step at a Time' (pages 28-34), but if we wanted to get the pony used to seeing pigs around, we may first of all put the pony in a pen 183m (200yd) from the pigs until the pony was relaxed about seeing them. Over a week or more, we may gradually move the pen closer to the pigs but only as much as the pony can reasonably stand. Incidentally, horses and ponies have good reason to be frightened of pigs; they often move in the very jerky fashion horses hate, but they also often bite. Never leave a horse or pony alone in the same space with pigs. It can be dangerous for the horses and the pigs.

### FLOODING

This is a far more dramatic version of habituation. It is important that the stimulus isn't stopped until the animal has totally calmed down, otherwise this may act to 'sensitize' the animal to the stimulus – the exact opposite of our intention. I do not recommend, particularly to a novice handler, ever putting themselves in the position to risk flooding a horse. It's also something I watch out for, and try to avoid, with any very sensitive horse, but particularly with Arabs who are not only sensitive but are also known as having incredible endurance. Whereas any other horse may take fright at something and overcome his fear within a few minutes, an Arab can keep his 'alarmed' state up for much longer. Avoidance where possible, and testing each new situation very carefully, is the route I prefer to take and is definitely a less traumatic option for horse and handler.

However, it's important to understand how flooding works. It means you're better informed as to the best decision to take if you ever find yourself taken by surprise with a horse that suddenly panics. Let us assume you are working on the ground and you have already read the Rules of Training (see pages 26-57), so you are in a perfectly safe, enclosed area. It may be that you are better off letting your horse fuss around for a while with his fear of long lines or spooking in an exaggerated fashion at something at the edge of the arena. Horses have to be fairly rapid learners. Most people accept that it's important for horses to know what's dangerous in order to enable them to dodge and flee from those things. This is an innate ability which has allowed the fittest to survive all these years. However, it's of equal importance that they are able to learn quickly what is not dangerous, otherwise they would have spent so much time dodging and fleeing they'd never have had time to eat. It's worth taking into consideration that in the wild the youngster is guided by the reactions of his mother and other herd members to whatever is going on. So if the horse starts going into a big fuss the first time the long lines touch him, or starts shying away at something new, if we, as a leading herd member, stay cool, very often the horse settles down remarkably quickly. This, in effect, is what Monty Roberts and I do when putting the first saddle on a youngster in the round pen. We let him loose to get used to the feeling of it, even have a buck and a kick if he so desires. We act unconcerned and as soon as he settles down, which usually takes less than a minute, we invite him back to us to tell him how good he is and continue with the process.

## PUT THE BEHAVIOUR ON CUE

To extinguish an unwanted behaviour you can teach that behaviour deliberately, and then not give the cue for it to be performed. This is why it's a good idea to teach your horse to back up, both when you are on the ground and when you are riding. Sometimes problems start when it's not taught: the horse takes a step back accidentally for some rea-

**FLOODING**

HORSES CAN LEARN QUICKLY WHAT IS NOT DANGEROUS AND SOON SETTLE DOWN WITH THE SADDLE.

son, he feels the rider 'freeze' for a second, and he thinks, 'Oh, this is an interesting move to make!' Suddenly the horse and not the rider 'owns' that direction. Make sure you have charge of all the directions, including backing up and lateral movements.

## TEACHING AN INCOMPATIBLE BEHAVIOUR

An incompatible behaviour is being miserable, for example, when singing 'Oh Happy Days'. I'm not suggesting instant cures for severe clinical disorders here but a way of altering general day-to-day emotions that can be affected by how we hold our bodies. If you want to 'do' bored, you will sit in a slumped position and your breathing will be shallow. Try to do 'fed up' or 'depressed' with your favourite dance music on. What about if you dance around and really take in some air? Admit you're happy. In Additional Yielding Exercises (see pages 74-85) we've already talked about how a horse having his head lowered is incompatible with him being nervous and worried.

## LATENT LEARNING

One of my favourites! One of the official definitions of latent learning is 'learning that is not demonstrated by behaviour at the time of learning but can be shown to have occurred by increasing the reinforcement for such behaviour'. Exact definitions vary for this. Another way it is generally explained is 'learning that has occurred which was not apparent at the time'. I was always aware of this as a teenager, being responsible for schooling a wide variety of ponies. I'd just never heard the proper term, so always wondered if these inexplicable improvements that would suddenly appear as if by magic only happened to me. Some days I'd be working with a pony – say, trying to get him to canter on the correct leg – and we'd be getting nowhere at all. Having always been a fairly philosophical character, I'd persevere for a while and in the end finish that schooling session as the pony accidentally came on the right leg or some such thing.

The next day I'd get going and the pony would be like: 'So, what is it? Left leg? Right leg? It's all simple to me!' Before hearing of latent learning I tried to explain it as 'horses seem to learn overnight or when resting'. A 'label' adds so much more credibility though; one of the reasons I wanted to do this chapter for you. Be aware of how this can happen with your horses, but also be aware that it happens with us as well, especially when you have challenges to face. It is necessary to do the initial work and consciously try hard to work things out; after that, you are best off taking a complete break and forgetting all about it for a while. Give your thoughts a chance to germinate and the flowering can take you by surprise. How many times have you had your best ideas in the bath? Eureka! Or in the shower? This was apparently Einstein's favourite spot for ideas. Driving? Steven Spielberg claims he gets his best ideas in the car.

## MIMICRY

In common with many animals horses are natural mimics. One of the greatest assets you can possess when you are starting young horses is that priceless object 'the schoolmaster'. He's not only excellent for teaching people to ride in safety but invaluable as a lead horse and trainer of your youngsters. There is nothing better than a 'good influence' at the start of a youngster's training. A wise, older horse can show him there is no need to be worried by traffic, puddles, dogs and, indeed, that there is no need for life to be anything other than a very pleasant, stress-free experience.

The lead horse can be useful for teaching your horse to go through water, past traffic, jump ditches – which is why drag hunting is such a great education and confidence-giver for young horses. It is totally in their nature to run in herds in this way. If you don't have a suitable lead horse, sometimes you will have to take on that role yourself. Showing the horse with your own calmness and confidence that life is a pleasant experience, not something to worry about. If you lack a little confidence yourself, the old 'as if' comes into practice once again. You need to play the role of a confident person, well enough to convince your horse. You can even pick the exact person and literally act their part. 'Today, I am going to be ... Clint Eastwood in *Dirty Harry*!'

Once the youngster has acquired this initial confidence, the time can come when he goes out on his own, and eventually becomes the lead horse himself. You need to read the situation, though, and not try and rush your youngster before he's ready. That won't make him braver; it'll just make him anxious. Take things one step at a time. Don't ask too much of him at once. Keep praising him and telling him how brave he is for every little effort.

On the flip side, I've also noticed youngsters pick up strange quirks from older horses with whom they're being ridden. I first noticed it when our lead horse for the racehorse yearlings did a rather unusual head twirl as she was being ridden along. Within a week all three yearlings going out with her had all managed to fit the same action into their repertoire. Also, be aware they have been known to watch humans and copy how to undo gate latches, doors and untie themselves. I've heard of people saying they've even known youngsters copy another horse's lameness or bad action. It sounds rather far-fetched but just watch out for this.

Remember, when you are around your horse, to make sure you are giving off the right signals because he'll take the lead in many ways from you. The more frightened and concerned he is, the more he needs

> Sometimes if you give a long sigh, the horse will copy you, relaxing him and often bringing a breakthrough in his training.

your reassurance by your actions and attitude that really there is nothing to worry about. A reaction I love to get from a horse when I'm training him is a nice sigh. It always signals to me that the horse is starting to relax. It means he's starting to make a commitment to the work in hand. It's not something you can rush, but sometimes if you give a long relaxed sigh at an appropriate time, the horse will copy you. This tension-relieving gesture is going to encourage both of you to relax and certainly can't do any harm - so don't forget to try it.

## LEARNED HELPLESSNESS

The concept of 'learned helplessness' was developed by psychologist Martin Seligman and his colleagues at the University of Pennsylvania. Beginning in the 1960s, they discovered that when dogs were administered unavoidable, inescapable shocks, eventually they just seemed to give up. Even when given a chance to escape – by being moved to a different cage with only a low barrier over which they could jump – they still acted helpless and continued to accept the shocks. These horrible experiments were the proof, if proof were needed, that if we are constantly in a 'no win' situation where we feel we have no control, after a while we'll just give up. A perception of security and control is very important to humans and to animals alike. Most people feel better if they have some money in the bank, their own home, and pension and health plans in place. I say 'a perception of security and control' because that's all it is – a perception. No matter how rich, successful and famous you are – cancer, car crashes and various other serious problems can arrive at anyone's door. You'll get better results with your horses if you don't try and force them but give them options. Make the option you'd like them to choose the easiest and most comfortable. In the same way, you wouldn't say to someone, 'Hey, you fetch that!' (At least I hope you wouldn't.) You'll get far more co-operative results if you say, 'Would you mind' to let them feel they had at least some say in the relationship. If you ever come across a 'depressed' horse, and they certainly do exist – I've even known of horses that will just lie down as soon as someone comes near them with a saddle – what you have to do is to give them 'wins', find them any little thing they can be successful at and give them lots of reward and praise. Don't be concerned about rewarding too much. Just concentrate on giving them a positive way forward.

I was discussing this idea of learned helplessness on one of my horse psychology weekends. A student was frowning through that whole part and it crossed my mind, 'Maybe she's thinking it's unlikely to happen with horses.' She came up to me in the break and said, 'About learned helplessness – I've been thinking. That's exactly how it is for us all at work – we're getting to the stage we think it's pointless trying because we're constantly in no-win situations.' She was trying to think up ways of getting her boss to come on a horse psychology weekend. She has since been in touch – she's left the job and feels a great sense of relief.

## DISPLACEMENT

Displacement refers to the shift of emotion away from the person or object towards which the bad feelings were originally felt to a more neutral or less dangerous person or object. For example, if you are told off by your boss but can't afford to lose your job, you don't risk upsetting him but suppress your anger at the time. You then go home and make life hell for everyone else. As a good friend of mine shrewdly noted: 'I'd hate to live on my own because then you'd have no one to blame if you were unhappy!'

Not infrequently, the smallest incident can serve as the trigger to release pent-up emotional feelings in a torrent of displaced anger and abuse. It can come in different guises: many a next-door neighbour has indulged in destructive and vindictive gossip as a means of expressing anger, resentment and hostility in their lives. So how is this relevant to horses, you may ask? The first, most important thing is that if we ever find ourselves angry or frustrated with a horse (probably because he's behaving like a horse – how dare he!), we need to look at ourselves first and think whether it's really the horse we are annoyed with or is it someone else in our lives. I think we are entitled to ask the same question of other people if we see them treating a horse unfairly, and try and help them and the horse. This isn't always easy. Horses are easy targets for bullies. They are flight animals and don't speak so they can't tell (any but the most observant listeners). A dog will squeal out in pain to let its feelings be known. Do people think that because horses don't cry out, they don't feel any pain? Or is it just easier not to think about it?

Displacement is relevant in horse behaviour as well. Many of the stable vices – box walking, weaving, windsucking and crib biting (nowadays often referred to as 'stereotypical vices') – are partly or mainly caused by displacement behaviour due to frustration. The activities they are engaged in may seem pointless or irrelevant but they do them out of frustration at not being able to do what they would really like. Licking and chewing may be read as 'a sign' but is it more likely to be unconsciously so as far as the horse is concerned and, in fact, a displacement behaviour caused by anxiety and/or not being sure how an approach will be accepted. This suckling gesture is a remnant of how a foal might approach his mother or older horses seeming to say, 'I'm just a little baby. I don't mean any harm. Please don't hurt me.' It's not a gesture that is exclusive to horses though. If you like to study human behaviour as well, you will have noticed the pulling in of cheeks and the distorted mouth movements often performed by people who are anxious or stressed.

> Who are you really angry at?
> Your horse?
> Your self?
> Or somebody else all together?

*Case study*

# A LATENT-LEARNING SUCCESS STORY

*As a teenager I had a former racehorse, Chesney (show name 'The Real Thing'). I was taking him showjumping to the Wales and West Show where I knew they had water ditches. I took him to one of our neighbours who had cross-country fences to 'try' him over their water ditch. This 'just trying him over the ditch' was going nowhere fast. He was convinced as soon as he saw the ditch that my only intention in getting him near must be to push him in and drown him. I've never liked hitting horses, even in those days, when people seemed to do it as a matter of course, so when we started getting near enough for him to refuse at the actual jump, I turned him in circles as a penalty and then tried to face him at it again. What a performance! Although throughout this he was barely warm, I have to confess after an hour of this I was exhausted. After another exaggerated veer away from the ditch, I didn't fall off, I sort of flopped off. Making the most of my short rest on the floor I mentioned to my sister, Sandra, who was helping me, that maybe it would be a good idea if we concentrated on the classes without water ditches. As she was legging me up again, I suggested hopefully that perhaps they wouldn't even include the water ditches at this show? She thought I should just jump him over something easy and then, in Scarlett O'Hara fashion, 'think about it tomorrow'.*

*With no real optimism at all, we went out to the field the next day and I jumped him over a few of the fences. I faced him at the ditch and asked him on ... and he popped over it as if he'd been doing it his whole life! He never had a problem with ditches again, either there or in the ring. He turned out to be a lovely horse.*

*If I were faced with the same problem today, as soon as I realized that a horse had a real aversion to anything I would break the problem down into easier steps. For instance, first of all get him to step over half a plastic guttering, and then half a plastic guttering with some water in it, and so on, and keep rewarding every success. I'd also consider getting a lead from a totally confident older horse in the early stages, or failing that I'd find a way to lead him over myself. Still, one of the things that make horses so addictive, is that there is so much to learn, and you can always improve and I certainly experienced a remarkable case of latent learning.*

## ANTHROPOMORPHISM

This originally meant attributing human personality to God but has since extended 'to God or animals'. Anthropomorphism is very much frowned upon by behaviourists and scientists.

For a detailed analysis of the differences between the beliefs and language of scientists, behaviourists and horse people (and in this context I would definitely put myself into the 'horse person' category), I don't believe you could do better than to read Lesley Skipper's excellent book *Inside Your Horse's Mind*, which explores this subject in depth. In her chapter 'The Great Heresy' she describes how to be accused of anthropomorphism is so taboo that in scientific speak, 'an animal cannot be said to be frightened; instead, it shows flight behaviour. It does not feel affection; it displays courtship or parental behaviour. It is not angry; it exhibits aggression. A horse is not curious; is shows investigative behaviour.' She continues: "So we are told that when an animal has voluntarily stopped drinking (in lieu of disturbing or distracting external stimuli) and has begun to engage in some other behaviour, we can usually infer that its water need had been satiated." In anthropomorphic terms, the animal is no longer "thirsty".'

Perhaps this language became necessary, in part, for scientists to justify some of the unpleasant experiments that they were performing on animals. If it is a fact that the subjects have no conscious thoughts or feelings, it must be much easier on one's conscience. To quote from Lesley Skipper once more: 'It is worthwhile recalling it is not so long ago in historical terms that many educated Europeans dismissed the physical and emotional sufferings of the poor, and of other races, with the belief (often genuinely held) that "they don't feel things as we do".'

I'm sure most of us are guilty of transferring our personalities on to our horses in some way or another. Whereas one person may tell you the horse has 'a sense of humour' and is 'just having a joke', another person may label the same horse 'cunning', 'evil' or 'dishonest'. Any psychologist will tell you that these labels say a great deal more about the human than the horse. Sadly, those really destructive labels can give you a negative attitude towards the horse that won't be any help at all in finding the right way forward.

There are many words that have been, perhaps, unfairly corrupted by misuse. 'Respect' is one such. Respect should only be a good thing but sadly some people's ideas of getting respect is by unacceptable behaviour. 'Animals rights' is another label that can often make people think first of letter bombs or violent protests but essentially is a good thing – animals should have rights. As in all things, a balanced outlook is necessary. Horses have different needs from us in many areas. How they are like humans is that every individual deserves to be treated with respect, no matter what his breed, colour, size or monetary worth.

> A group of scientists taught a spider to jump on the word command 'Up!' They decided to test what would happen if they cut all his legs off. They shouted 'Up!' but the spider didn't jump. The scientists concluded that 'cutting the spider's legs off had caused him to go deaf'.

Studies done recently have shown that animals do experience love, jealousy and grief as well as a host of other 'human' qualities, and obviously putting things into human terms and human language makes it far easier for us to explain things coming from our own understanding. I like the concept of 'selective anthropomorphism' a term coined, I believe, by author Dr Marte Kiley-Worthington. While we frown on people who use negative terms such as 'this horse is being deliberately annoying', we unashamedly recount how our horse was at the show and 'he really did his best because he wanted to win' and was 'so proud of himself when he got the rosette'. Hypocrites? Certainly not – we're selective anthropomorphists!

## AND NOW LET'S TALK ABOUT OUR MANNERS
Because little things really do mean a lot.

**Perfect manners.** Don't ignore your horse when you go to see him in the mornings. Always say a polite 'Good morning, Tom' (or whatever his name) when you go to see him. The actual greeting may not matter but all horses are quite capable of recognizing their name and should be encouraged to do so. The most important thing is not to creep silently up on your horse and surprise him.

**Perfect manners.** Don't go in to see your horse with your head buzzing about all the other things you have to do and carrying over negative 'baggage' that involves other people. Make being with your horse at that time, in that space the most important thing in your life at that moment. Clear your mind before you go over him and give him your full attention.

**Perfect manners.** Make sure that whenever you go to your horse he receives a greeting stroke first. Don't just go in and grab some part of his anatomy – a leg, or his tail, say. This can prevent you getting kicked as well, which we don't want to happen (even if you deserve it).

**Perfect manners.** Don't give horses derogatory names or allow others to do so. Labelling a horse 'stupid' or 'a bitch' gives other people the impression it is all right to treat those horses in an unfeeling and disrespectful way and doesn't really give the horse a chance. Take careful note and you will see that it is often the owners of such horses that deserve the label more than the horses. Lest you be judged in this way, it may be better to label your horse by his more positive features, or describe him or her as 'unflappable' or 'very sensitive'.

**Perfect manners.** Don't be rude by thumping your tack on to your horse, trying to fold his ears over to put the bridle on, putting an ice-cold bit in his mouth or hoicking the girths up. Remember, horses are sensitive.

**Perfect manners.** It is your duty to learn to ride as well as you possibly can, supporting your bodyweight in the most comfortable way possible for your horse.

**Perfect manners.** Don't use your horse as a full-time grandstand, sitting in a slumped position for hours at horse shows or meetings.

**Perfect manners.** If a foreigner doesn't understand your language, it is rude to speak more loudly at them in exasperation. In the same way learn as much of your horse's language as you possibly can. Try to look at situations in the way that he may look at them.

**Perfect manners.** Don't just expect your horse to know what you want him to do and then blame him for the fact that you hadn't taught him to do it.

And remember that everything you do to create a friendly, supportive atmosphere in the yard and elsewhere is going to be picked up by the horses and make them feel better, so:

**Don't be rude** by giving other people's horses (or children) titbits or treats without permission.

**Don't be rude** – don't even begin to think of hitting someone else's horse (or children).

**Don't be rude** by letting your children run around the back legs of other people's horses and then complain when they get kicked.

**Don't be rude** if you have a groom always introduce him or her when people come into the yard or when they are showing horses for people. If you are shown a horse by a groom always acknowledge their presence and thank them. Tips are also appreciated if someone has put in a lot of extra effort for you in a racing, hunting or showing yard.

**Don't be rude** if you ride somebody else's horse – unless they already have help arranged – always groom or wipe the horse down, check his feet, put his rugs on (if appropriate), and put the tack away tidily. They may say you don't need to bother, but they will appreciate it.

**Don't be rude** if you are a groom always make eye contact with anyone coming into the yard and smile and introduce yourself if appropriate. Ask whoever's in charge what they would like you to say if someone you don't know comes into the yard. This will make an enormous difference to the whole atmosphere and how people perceive the yard, making it a nicer, more relaxed place for the horses as well.

**Don't be rude** 'DIY' yards are a minefield of upset feelings if lines of communication are not kept clear. If you are in charge of a DIY yard, suggest regular meetings. This way people can air any minor differences before they get into a full-blown battle. If you are a new owner at a DIY yard, find a time to meet the other owners. Ask if there are any rules, written or unwritten. Ask what time other people feed their horses. Will it upset them if you feed your horse earlier/later? Make every effort to be friendly and ensure you are all working together for the benefit of the horses.

**Don't be rude** – if someone appears to be having a problem with a horse, ask them, 'Would you like any help?' If they say, 'No, thank you very much', go away and leave them alone. There is nothing worse if you want to spend a minute or two getting your horse to stand still as you get on, or if he just hesitates at the horsebox, than having people interfering and making you feel that you've got to hurry.

**Don't be rude** just because you are the best rider at your stables, or even if the best rider in the county, it doesn't mean that you are a better human being in the great cosmic plan of the universe. Yes, some people may not ride as well as you. Some people may even be nervous. Don't act or even feel superior to them – they may be ten times more intelligent than you in every other way. Let's face it – you don't have to be a brain surgeon to ride a horse.

**Don't be rude** and criticize another person's horse unless they have specifically asked for your opinion. Horses literally become 'part of the family'. Making negative observations about someone's horse is on a par with pointing out their husband has boss eyes or child has bow legs. You may feel very clever observing, 'Oh, your new horse has cow hocks', but don't expect any sympathy from me if they then growl back, 'I would have thought you would be the last person that should be criticizing anyone's legs, dearie!'

**Don't be rude** – when driving a car always slow down for horses and give them a wide berth.

**Don't be rude** – drivers have rights as well. When riding always wave and smile at drivers whether they slow down or not – at least they might feel guilty enough to slow down next time, thought admittedly it is hard to smile and wave when you are actually being run over.

**Don't be rude** when you are driving so slowly (or should be) with your trailer attached and look like the Pied Piper of Hamelin with a long queue of traffic behind; do pull over occasionally to generate good will for horse owners.

**JUST PICK UP THE PHONE**
IF YOU STILL FEEL YOU NEED HELP, CALL THE INTELLIGENT HORSEMANSHIP ASSOCIATION FOR ADVICE (SEE OVERLEAF).

**Don't be rude** when you are riding always give pedestrians a wide berth and smile and say hello. Remember, it's very easy to look arrogant if you are sitting on a horse, high above everyone else. Pedestrians often feel very vulnerable as horses walk by, particularly if they are nervous or unfamiliar with horses as well.

**Don't be rude** – make good manners and consideration a way of life. Don't expect your farrier to walk a mile to catch your muddy horse and then let him or her work in the rain with no one to hold the horse. Don't speak to show secretaries on the phone as if they are idiots. When you go into your tack shop (indeed any shop), acknowledge the person serving and say 'thank you' as you leave. Remember that everywhere you go, even on the end of phone lines, there are real human beings with hopes, dreams, disappointments; their lives are just waiting for you to bring a little joy into them – so take every chance you can to make everyone's day that little bit better.

**Don't be rude** – whenever you get off somebody else's horse, or if you have had any dealing with somebody else's horse, you should always, always find something nice to say about that horse. Remember, somebody, somewhere loves that horse. And if they don't? Well, in that case it's even more important.

**Note:** If you feel it would be rude to tell anyone they need to take note of these suggestions, then buy them this book for Christmas.

## USEFUL ADDRESSES

For information on Intelligent Horsemanship courses, demonstrations and merchandise worldwide see our web site: **www.intelligenthorsemanship.co.uk**

or write to:
**Kelly Marks**
Intelligent Horsemanship
Lethornes
Lambourn
Berkshire RG17 8QS
Telephone: (+44) 01488 71300 or fax: (+44) 01488 73783

## AUTHOR'S ACKNOWLEDGMENTS

Many thanks to Ian Vandenberghe, Angela Vince and my sister, Sandra O'Halloran who in particular have been driving forces in my life, convincing me I am capable of far more than I would have believed. Thanks to all my past and present students, now great friends and associates, for their help and advice, especially Nicole Golding on the literary side who is soon to write her own book. Also Linda Ruffle, Dido Fisher, Julia Scholes, Sylvia Arnold and Jayne Hopkinson, who are such a help and support and all my students whose case studies have been included. Thanks to Brenda Whelehan for her wonderful organisation of the office and Jess Wallace and Jane Young for their excellent photographs. Thanks to John Beaton, who came up with the idea for this book. Henrietta Knight and Charlie Edwards are among people who have been postive influences in my time with horses. Finally, enormous thanks are due to Monty Roberts whose generosity and inspiration in putting me on the path to Intelligent Horsemanship has been immeasurable.

# INDEX

Page numbers in *italic* refer to the illustrations